Modern Tragedy

FORMS OF DRAMA

Forms of Drama meets the need for accessible, mid-length volumes that offer undergraduate readers authoritative guides to the distinct forms of global drama. From classical Greek tragedy to Chinese pear garden theatre, cabaret to *kathakali*, the series equips readers with models and methodologies for analysing a wide range of performance practices and engaging with these as 'craft'.

SERIES EDITOR: SIMON SHEPHERD

Badhai: Hijra-Khwaja Sira-Trans *Performance across Borders in South Asia*
978-1-3501-7453-5
Adnan Hossain, Claire Pamment and Jeff Roy

Cabaret
978-1-3501-4025-7
William Grange

Classical Greek Tragedy
978-1-3501-4456-9
Judith Fletcher

The Commedia dell'Arte
978-1-3501-4418-7
Domenico Pietropaolo

Liyuanxi – Chinese 'Pear Garden Theatre'
978-1-3501-5739-2
Josh Stenberg

Pageant
978-1-3501-4451-4
Joan FitzPatrick Dean

Romantic Comedy
978-1-3501-8337-7
Trevor R. Griffiths

Satire
978-1-3501-4007-3
Joel Schechter

Tragicomedy
978-1-3501-4430-9
Brean Hammond

Modern Tragedy

James Moran

methuen | drama

LONDON • NEW YORK • OXFORD • NEW DELHI • SYDNEY

METHUEN DRAMA
Bloomsbury Publishing Plc
50 Bedford Square, London, WC1B 3DP, UK
1385 Broadway, New York, NY 10018, USA
29 Earlsfort Terrace, Dublin 2, Ireland

BLOOMSBURY, METHUEN DRAMA and the Methuen Drama logo are trademarks of Bloomsbury
Publishing Plc

First published in Great Britain 2023

Series design by Charlotte Daniels

A catalogue record for this book is available from the British Library.

Library of Congress Cataloging-in-Publication Data
Names: Moran, James, 1978- author.
Title: Modern tragedy / James Moran.
Description: London ; New York : Methuen Drama 2023. | Series: Forms of drama |
Includes bibliographical references and index. |
Summary: "What distinguishes modern tragedy from other forms of drama? How does it
relate to contemporary political and social conditions? To what ends have artists employed the tragic
form in different locations during the 20th century? The first chapter of this book is motivated by the
urgency of our current situation in an age of ecocidal crisis. It focuses upon John Millington Synge's
Riders to the Sea (1904), and shows how environmental awareness might be expressed through
tragic drama. The second chapter takes a detailed look at Brecht's reworking of Synge's drama
in the 1937 play Señora Carrar's Rifles. Examining Brecht's script in the light of his broader ideas
about tragedy, this study notes that Brecht felt earlier tragedies tended to leave their audiences
emotionally stimulated but stunted in terms of political understanding and response. This chapter
highlights how Brecht's ideas of tragedy were informed by Hegel and Marx, and contrasts Brecht's
approach with the Schopenhauerian thinking of Samuel Beckett. The third chapter examines theatre
makers whose ideas were partly motivated by applying an understanding of the tragic narrative of
Synge's Riders to the Sea to postcolonial contexts. This part of the book looks at Derek Walcott's
The Sea at Dauphin (1954), and J.P. Clark's The Goat (1961). It explores how tragedy, a form that
is often associated with regressive assumptions about hegemony, might be rethought, and how
aspects of the tragic may coincide with the experiences and concerns of non-white
authors and audiences"– Provided by publisher.
Identifiers: LCCN 2022029808 | ISBN 9781350139770 (paperback) |
ISBN 9781350139787 (hardback) | ISBN 9781350139794 (epub) |
ISBN 9781350139800 (ebook) | ISBN 9781350139817
Subjects: LCSH: Tragedy–History and criticism. | Drama–History and criticism.
Classification: LCC PN1897 .M66 2023 | DDC 809.2/512–dc23/eng/20220929
LC record available at https://lccn.loc.gov/2022029808

ISBN: HB: 978-1-3501-3978-7
            PB: 978-1-3501-3977-0
            ePDF: 978-1-3501-3980-0
            eBook: 978-1-3501-3979-4

Series: Forms of Drama

Typeset by Integra Software Services Pvt. Ltd.
Printed and bound in Great Britain

To find out more about our authors and books visit www.bloomsbury.com and sign up for our
newsletters.

CONTENTS

Series Preface vi
Acknowledgements xi

Introduction: Does modern tragedy exist? 1

1 From 1904: Synge and the nature elegy 31

2 From 1937: Brecht and political engagement 61

3 From 1954: Walcott, Clark, and the postcolonial 95

Conclusion 125

Notes 130
Bibliography 157
Index 169

SERIES PREFACE

The scope of this series is scripted aesthetic activity that works by means of personation.

Scripting is done in a wide variety of ways. It may, most obviously, be the more or less detailed written text familiar in the stage play of the Western tradition, which provides not only lines to be spoken but directions for speaking them. Or it may be a set of instructions, a structure or scenario, on the basis of which performers improvise, drawing, as they do so, on an already learnt repertoire of routines and responses. Or there may be nothing written, just sets of rules, arrangements and even speeches orally handed down over time. The effectiveness of such unwritten scripting can be seen in the behaviour of audiences, who, without reading a script, have learnt how to conduct themselves appropriately at the different activities they attend. For one of the key things that unwritten script specifies and assumes is the relationship between the various groups of participants, including the separation, or not, between doers and watchers.

What is scripted is specifically an aesthetic activity. That specification distinguishes drama from non-aesthetic activity using personation. Following the work of Erving Goffman in the mid-1950s, especially his book *The Presentation of Self in Everyday Life*, the social sciences have made us richly aware of the various ways in which human interactions are performed. Going shopping, for example, is a performance in that we present a version of ourselves in each encounter we make. We may indeed have changed our clothes before setting out. This, though, is a social performance.

The distinction between social performance and aesthetic activity is not clear-cut. The two sorts of practice overlap and mingle with one another. An activity may be more or less aesthetic, but the crucial distinguishing feature is the status of the aesthetic element. Going shopping may contain an aesthetic element – decisions about clothes and shoes to wear – but its purpose is not deliberately to make an aesthetic activity or to mark itself as different from everyday social life. The aesthetic element is not regarded as a general requirement. By contrast a court-room trial may be seen as a social performance, in that it has an important social function, but it is at the same time extensively scripted, with prepared speeches, costumes and choreography. This scripted aesthetic element assists the social function in that it conveys a sense of more than everyday importance and authority to proceedings which can have life-changing impact. Unlike the activity of going shopping the aesthetic element here is not optional. Derived from tradition it is a required component that gives the specific identity to the activity.

It is defined as an activity in that, in a way different from a painting of Rembrandt's mother or a statue of Ramesses II, something is made to happen over time. And, unlike a symphony concert or firework display, that activity works by means of personation. Such personation may be done by imitating and interpreting – 'inhabiting' – other human beings, fictional or historical, and it may use the bodies of human performers or puppets. But it may also be done by a performer who produces a version of their own self, such as a stand-up comedian or court official on duty, or by a performer who, through doing the event, acquires a self with special status as with the *hijras* securing their sacredness by doing the ritual practice of *badhai*.

Some people prefer to call many of these sorts of scripted aesthetic events not drama but cultural performance. But there are problems with this. First, such labelling tends to keep in place an old-fashioned idea of Western scholarship that drama, with its origins in ancient Greece, is a specifically European 'high' art. Everything outside it is then potentially, and damagingly, consigned to a domain which may be neither 'art' nor 'high'. Instead the European stage play and its like can best be regarded as a subset of the general category, distinct from the rest in that two groups of people come together in order specifically to present and watch a story being acted out by imitating other persons and settings. Thus the performance of a stage play in this tradition consists of two levels of activity using personation: the interaction of audience and performers and the interaction between characters in a fictional story.

The second problem with the category of cultural performance is that it downplays the significance and persistence of script, in all its varieties. With its roots in the traditional behaviours and beliefs of a society script gives specific instructions for the form – the materials, the structure and sequence – of the aesthetic activity, the drama. So too, as we have noted, script defines the relationships between those who are present in different capacities at the event.

It is only by attending to what is scripted, to the form of the drama, that we can best analyse its functions and pleasures. At its most simple analysis of form enables us to distinguish between different sorts of aesthetic activity. The masks used in *kathakali* look different from those used in *commedia dell'arte*. They are made of different materials, designs, and colours. The roots of those differences lie in their separate cultural traditions and systems of living. For similar reasons the puppets of *karagoz* and *wayang* differ. But perhaps more importantly the attention to form provides a basis for exploring the operation and effects of a particular work. Those who regularly participate in and watch drama, of whatever sort, learn to recognize and remember the forms of what they see and hear. When one drama has family resemblances to another, in its organization and use of materials, structure and sequences, those who attend it develop expectations as to how it will – or indeed should – operate. It then becomes possible to specify how a particular work subverts, challenges or enhances these expectations.

Expectation doesn't only govern response to individual works, however. It can shape, indeed has shaped, assumptions about which dramas are worth studying. It is well established that Asia has ancient and rich dramatic traditions, from the Indian sub-continent to Japan, as does Europe, and these are studied with enthusiasm. But there is much less widespread activity, at least in Western universities, in relation to the traditions of, say, Africa, Latin America and the Middle East. Secondly, even within the recognized traditions, there are assumptions that some dramas are more 'artistic', or indeed more 'serious', 'higher' even, than others. Thus it may be assumed that *noh* or classical tragedy will require the sort of close attention to craft which is not necessary for mumming or *badhai*.

Both sets of assumptions here keep in place a system which allocates value. This series aims to counteract a discriminatory value system by ranging as widely as possible across world practices and by giving the same sort of attention to all the forms it features. Thus book-length studies of forms such as *al-halqa*, *hana keaka*, and *ta'zieh* will appear in English for perhaps the first time. Those studies, just like those of *kathakali*, tragicomedy and the rest, will adopt the same basic approach. That approach consists of an historical overview of the development of a form combined with, indeed anchored in, detailed analysis of examples and case studies. One of the benefits of properly detailed analysis is that it can reveal the construction which gives a work the appearance of being serious, artistic, and indeed 'high'.

What does that work of construction is script. This series is grounded in the idea that all forms of drama have script of some kind and that an understanding of drama, of any sort, has to include analysis of that script. In taking this approach, books in this series again challenge an assumption which has in recent times governed the study of drama. Deriving from the supposed, but artificial, distinction between cultural performance and drama, many accounts of cultural performance ignore its scriptedness and assume that the proper way of studying it is simply to describe how its practitioners behave and what they make. This is useful enough, but to leave it at that is to produce something that looks like a form of lesser anthropology. The description of behaviours is only the first step in that it establishes what the script is. The next step is to analyse how the script and form work and how they create effect.

But it goes further than this. The close-up analyses of materials, structures, and sequences – of scripted forms – show how they emerge from and connect deeply back into the modes of life and belief to which they are necessary. They tell us in short why, in any culture, the drama needs to be done. Thus by adopting the extended model of drama, and by approaching all dramas in the same way, the books in this series aim to tell us why, in all societies, the activities of scripted aesthetic personation – dramas – keep happening, and need to keep happening.

I am grateful, as always, to Mick Wallis for helping me to think through these issues. Any clumsiness or stupidity is entirely my own.

Simon Shepherd

ACKNOWLEDGEMENTS

I would like to express my thanks to Janette Dillon, Mark Dudgeon, and Fifi Edem for all of their generous assistance with this volume. I am thankful to my own colleagues and students at the University of Nottingham and, further back in time, at Downing College, for allowing me to rehearse a number of the ideas that appear here. During recent months I have been particularly thankful to Chris Collins, Steve Giles, Brean Hammond, and Simon Shepherd for their generous comments on draft material. I'm not at all thankful to Covid-19, as the arrival of that particular virus caused quite a delay with completing the manuscript, but I am very grateful to Lara Bateman and Ella Wilson for proving very understanding and flexible about deadlines. As always, I'm grateful to Maria, Thomas, and Joseph for everything else.

Excerpts from Samuel Beckett's 'Whoroscope Notebook' (Reading University Library) reproduced by kind permission of the Estate of Samuel Beckett c/o Rosica Colin Limited, London. The manuscript material of Samuel Beckett is also published here by permission of the University of Reading, Beckett International Foundation.

Introduction: Does modern tragedy exist?

Millions of people have perished since the start of the twentieth century. Between then and now, the world has witnessed many notorious examples of famine, war, and genocide. The period has seen the dropping of the atomic bomb, mass deaths on the Killing Fields of Cambodia, and the horrors of the Nazi concentration camps. Certainly, this era has been replete with numerous examples of 'tragedy' as we might understand the term in everyday conversation, as a word that indicates something involving great sorrow, suffering, and bereavement. Yet numerous commentators have noted that during this time, tragedy, in a more artistic sense, has not really happened at all.

In his 1961 study, *The Death of Tragedy*, George Steiner declared modern tragedy impossible. For Steiner, tragedy simply could not exist in a secular age when the gods had been knocked from their perch, when the heroes of myth had lost their influence, and when the heightened language of the theatre stage had been displaced by speech that was humdrum and workaday. 'Given the abuses of language by political terror and by the illiteracy of mass consumption, can we look to a return of that mystery in words which lies at the source of tragic poetry?', asked Steiner, before answering, 'I think not'.[1] In the 1990s he continued: 'it is difficult to imagine a renascence of high tragic theatre in a positivistic climate of consciousness, in a mass-market society, more and more of whose thinking members regard the question of the existence of God, let alone of demonic agents intervening in mundane affairs, as archaic nonsense'.[2]

Steiner was thinking here of a literary idea of tragedy which coincides with, but avoids mapping neatly onto, any wider use of the term, either in vernacular use or in philosophical discourse. As Patrice Pavis warns, 'We must be careful to distinguish between *tragedy*, a literary genre having its own rules, and the *tragic*, an anthropological and philosophical principle'. But such notions are continually colliding and intersecting, as Pavis then acknowledges by observing, 'the tragic is clearly best studied in tragedies'.[3] The starting point for the literary notion of 'tragedy' is shrouded in mystery, and even the origins of the term are obscure. 'Tragedy' is, for some reason, derived from Greek words for 'goat' and 'song'. Although the earliest ritual developments are lost, there was an astonishing flourishing of tragic plays at public festivals in ancient Greece during the fifth century BCE. These dramas tell of the heroes of legend and religion, describe events in elevated language, and often consist of narratives that end badly for the protagonists: although by contrast with later ideas about tragedy, the tragedies performed 2,500 years ago sometimes concluded with characters escaping from threatened doom. The large, open-air performance festivals in ancient Greece produced a great deal of tragedy that has since been lost, and we have complete plays by only three ancient Athenian tragedians, Aeschylus (*c*.525–456 BCE), Sophocles (*c*.496–406 BCE), and Euripides (*c*.480–406 BCE).

The ancient Greek performances look far removed from today's ideas of theatre. As John J. Winkler and Froma I. Zeitlin stated in 1990, 'The more we learn about the original production of tragedies and comedies in Athens, the more it seems wrong even to call them plays in the modern sense of the word'.[4] Attic drama depended on the chanting of choral odes, involved masked actors and an all-male audience, and incorporated a series of conventions that would look relatively alien to most modern spectators. Winkler has suggested of the major theatre festival held in ancient Athens:

The opening event of the City Dionysia was the ephebes' [young soldiers'] re-enactment of the advent of Dionysus, which included a sacrifice at a hearth-altar (eskhara) near the Academy, a torchlight procession with the cult statue, and (perhaps on the next day, as part of the general barbecue) their sacrifice of a bull on behalf of the whole city. The daylight parade was a lavish spectacle – red-robed metics (resident aliens), phalluses and other precious religious objects carried by priests and honoured citizens, twenty dithyrambic choruses (ten of fifty boys each and ten of first men each) in their elaborate and expensive costumes.[5]

Today, relatively few plays begin with spectators ceremonially bearing their phalluses into the theatre. So can tragedy still exist in a modern society? George Steiner was scarcely the only thinker who felt that the answer to the question was a resounding no.

Over a century before Steiner made his argument, Hegel famously lamented in his *Lectures on Aesthetics* (published posthumously in 1835) that, because of societal evolution, 'The beautiful days of Greek art, like the golden age of the late Middle Ages, are gone'.[6] In similar vein, Nietzsche argued in *The Birth of Tragedy* (1872) that, following the lamentable interventions of Euripides and Sophocles, only a 'degenerate form of tragedy lived on, as a monument to her laborious and violent demise'.[7] Appropriately enough, for a form that often takes death as its subject matter, twentieth-century critics have also wondered whether tragedy itself has expired.

For example, in 1910, the philosopher György Lukács, when a relatively young man, argued that the modern tendency towards theatrical realism was fundamentally incompatible with tragedy. He observed that real life was lived in a rich variety of experiences: 'Life is an anarchy of light and dark: nothing is ever completely fulfilled in life, nothing ever quite ends; new, confusing voices always mingle with the chorus of those that have been heard before'.[8] By contrast, in the stage world, there is an essential falseness, where:

> there is only one person who speaks [...] while the other merely answers. But the one begins and the other ends, and the quiet, imperceptible flux of their relationship with one another, which real life alone can really bring to life, becomes lifeless and rigid in the harsh process of the dramatic description.[9]

Hence, a problem arose when modern drama moved towards realism, because lived experience had very little to do with the fixed rules of the playhouse, and, as Lukács saw it, 'Realism is bound to destroy all the form-creating and life-maintaining values of tragic drama'.[10]

During the interwar years, Walter Benjamin also wrote that tragic drama was a thing of the past. He felt that the 'modern theatre has nothing to show which remotely resembles the tragedy of the Greeks'.[11] However, unlike Lukács, who blamed theatrical realism, Benjamin pointed the finger at Christianity. The Christian religion had replaced tragedy with a rather more comic idea of salvation. As Brean Hammond puts it, 'If there is a benign deity, and there is an afterlife in which redeemed souls enjoy unbounded felicity, tragedies ending in piles of corpses are not the end of the story'.[12] Benjamin therefore writes:

> Stoic equanimity is fundamentally distinguished from Christian resignation by the fact that it teaches only calm endurance and unruffled expectation of unalterably necessary evils, but Christianity teaches renunciation, the giving up of willing. In just the same way the tragic heroes of the ancients show resolute and stoical subjection under the unavoidable blows of fate; the Christian tragedy, on the other hand, shows the giving up of the whole will to live, cheerful abandonment of the world in the consciousness of its worthlessness and vanity.[13]

Instead of tragedy, Benjamin identified *Trauerspiel* [sometimes translated as 'mourning drama'] in later theatre. For Benjamin, *Trauerspiel* ran along a different track to the tragic, combining Christian notions of suffering and sacrifice along with feelings of melancholy and abjection, and aligned less with myth than with events of history.

In a similar vein, Albert Camus asked, 'is modern tragedy possible?' His 1955 lecture 'On the Future of Tragedy' argues that:

> great periods of tragic art occur, in history, in centuries of crucial change, at moments when the life of peoples is heavy both with glory and with threats, when the future is uncertain and the present dramatic. After all, Aeschylus fought in two wars, and Shakespeare was contemporary to quite a remarkable succession of horrors.[14]

Camus looked at the ancient Greek and the Shakespearean ages and concluded that 'there have been only two periods of tragic art, both of which are narrowly defined in both time and space'.[15] 'Between those two tragic moments lie almost twenty centuries. During those twenty centuries, there was nothing at all, nothing', he emphasized, and – although the twentieth century was indeed marked by all kinds of war and radical social change – the idea of a tragic drama in modern times remained a 'dream', a 'hope', or as something that could be discerned only in 'the first tentative movements in this direction'.[16]

In the 1960s, Lucien Goldmann asserted that, even amongst the ancient dramatists, few of them had really been producing tragic works of art. He argued that Sophocles, whose extant scripts refuse to offer comforting resolutions, 'is the only one of the Greek playwrights who can, without any shadow of a doubt, be called "tragic"'.[17] Goldmann did focus upon articulations of tragedy in the seventeenth and eighteenth centuries, but felt that things had since significantly changed and that, by the mid-twentieth century, tragedy had been displaced by a different philosophical and artistic approach. Goldmann writes that 'it is in periods of social and political crisis that men are most aware of the enigma of their presence in the world. In the past, this awareness has tended to find its expression in tragedy. At the present day it shows itself in existentialism'.[18]

In any case, by the mid-twentieth century, how could theatrical representations of suffering continue as before 1945? As Theodor Adorno famously put it in 1949, 'to write poetry after Auschwitz is barbaric'.[19] Adorno felt that the twentieth century produced existential writing that was incompatible with tragedy, and stated that 'The expansion of the vulgar to the totality has meanwhile swallowed up what once laid claim to the noble and sublime: This is one of the reasons for the liquidation of the tragic'.[20] Figures like Goldmann and Camus argued that only in periods where the Roman candle of history fizzes with incident can tragedy be written. But, for Adorno, a different argument pertained: the sheer scale of real-life tragedy, and the vulgarity of modernity, had overwhelmed the basis of the work of art, and made tragic form look irrelevant. In an essay of 1967, Adorno highlighted the work of one writer in particular: 'In the face of Beckett's plays especially, the category of the tragic surrenders to laughter'.[21]

Thus Samuel Beckett's work served to highlight the pointlessness of striving for a tragic art form in an era that followed the Holocaust. As Rónán McDonald explains, Adorno had scarcely been alone in seeing Beckett's theatre as failing to correlate with traditional notions of tragedy. McDonald himself does include extensive discussion of Beckett's playwriting in an academic book about tragedy, but also acknowledges that 'even the most ecumenical definitions of tragedy are liable to have difficulty with Beckett's drama, which seems too diffuse, too concerned with the uncertain and the remorselessly squalid, to reach tragic status'.[22]

By the 1970s, Jean-Paul Sartre concluded that tragedy was not simply absent, but also frankly unwelcome: 'Tragedy, for us, is a historical phenomenon that triumphed between the sixteenth and eighteenth centuries. And we have no desire to revive it'.[23] In more recent years, an increasingly diverse range of figures have repeatedly argued that, if not already dead, tragedy ought to be euthanized. As Dympna Callaghan argued in 1989, 'The "universal" subject of liberal humanist tragic aesthetics is always male'.[24] Such thinking recently prompted P.A. Skantze to write:

> Though most of us (who are not straight white males) by necessity have learned to borrow a straight white male character's sorrow and make it our own, many of the traditional stories fuelling the downfall or the mistake or the misfortune of the hero are so sexist, so racist as to bar the female, queer, black/brown spectator from inhabiting the reversal and the recognition.[25]

Those of us who teach theatrical tragedy at university have found our students often expressing revulsion at the misogynistic and patriarchal aspects of many texts on the reading list, and educators quite rightly ask questions about how these scripts are framed, presented, and disseminated, as well as how such written works may appear to the members of groups and communities who suffer from various kinds of oppression and inequality. Such debates have profoundly affected my own teaching and thinking, although one thoughtful reaction is offered by Jennifer Wallace, who argues that it is precisely the persistence of twenty-first-century injustices that ensures the continuing relevance of the tragic. Wallace makes the case that 'Tragedy, by opening us up to a recognition of the precarious situation of others, whether or not we can explain it or justify it on a rational basis, produces bonds of interdependence and reciprocity'.[26]

Paradoxically, those critics whose names are mentioned above, and whose ideas about the death of tragedy are most familiar, are also the figures who have devoted some of the most careful thought to identifying and analysing tragedy, and whose writings have ensured that such a notoriously slippery and ill-defined term continues to have considerable purchase. Many of those thinkers have argued that, as an art, tragedy is dead, yet their prose has continued to give new life and energy to the subject. Today, the term 'tragedy' appears frequently in daily usage and has a prominent position in cultural debate. Few will raise an eyebrow when a political leader sends 'My prayers and condolences to the victims and families of the terrible tragedy'.[27] But in academic discourse, 'tragedy' has also maintained a pre-eminence across the twentieth century and beyond. The Cambridge academic I.A. Richards, in his 1924 book *The Principles of Literary Criticism*, asserted that tragedy was:

> still the form under which the mind may most clearly and freely contemplate the human situation, its issues unclouded, its possibilities revealed. To this its value is due and the supreme position among the arts which it has occupied in historical times and still occupies [...] Tragedy is too great an exercise of the spirit to be classed among amusements or even delights, or to be regarded as a vehicle for the inculcation of such crude valuations as may be codified in a moral.[28]

Long evenings in England's gloomy fens may very well have been more cheerily spent in the study of comic literature, but at Cambridge University, students studying English have been compelled to take an exam paper on 'Tragedy' ever since 1926.[29] One of the students who took that paper, Terry Eagleton, describes how, in his subsequent academic career, he went on to write extensively about tragedy 'perhaps because there are few other places where great art and the most fundamental moral and political issues are so closely intertwined'.[30] In the landmark study, *Tragedy and Dramatic Theatre* (published in German in 2014, English in 2016), Hans-Thies Lehmann suggests that, more widely, 'A definition of tragedy has been pursued more zealously throughout the ages than just about any other non-religious matter'.[31]

It is therefore necessary to sketch out, in brief at least, some of the major pre-twentieth-century developments in thinking about tragedy, as modern playwrights have repeatedly found themselves in dialogue or disagreement with those earlier ideas. Of course, critical interest in tragedy has scarcely been uniform across the centuries. In ancient Greece, Plato apparently wrote tragedies as a young man, and the dramatic form of his dialogues owes an evident debt to the theatrical world, but his philosophical writings frown on tragic verse because of the potentially damaging effect of such poetic work.[32] According to books 3 and 10 of Plato's *Republic*, the audience's appreciation of events that are manifestly untrue, that potentially show the gods in a bad light, and that reveal characters being motivated by emotions such as anger, lust, and desire rather than by reason, meant that tragedy should be excluded from the ideal city state. Plato observed that 'those who take up tragic poetry, whether in iambic or epic verse, are above all imitators' and 'the imitator knows nothing worth mentioning about the objects he's portraying, but that imitation is a kind of game and not serious'.[33]

Plato was answered by his student Aristotle, whose *Poetics* provides the Western world's foundational piece of literary theory. As Aristotle saw it, tragedy might have a beneficial effect, by allowing audiences to purge their emotions. He paid close attention to the key elements of Sophocles' play *Oedipus Rex*, and in this analysis, Aristotle provided several key terms including *pathos* (suffering); *hamartia* (a mistake, sometimes labelled the 'tragic flaw'); *peripeteia* (a reversal of fortune); and *anagnorisis* (a recognition of that changed state). These terms have been memorized by generations of students and widely cited as part of a search for governing rules that might define all tragedies without regard to content. Of particular influence, and some debate, has been Aristotle's ill-defined and briefly mentioned concept of 'catharsis', the notion that tragedy will arouse feelings of pity or fear, and will therefore allow a kind of psychological purifying. He posits the idea that by raising such feelings in dramatic form, the spectator may experience a sort of washing away of those feelings, and thus be calmed. Aristotle felt that unhappy endings were best, as those would elicit the appropriate emotional response, an idea that was contested in the fourth century BCE but which would have a powerful influence on later thinking about the genre. Yet Aristotle scarcely expressed enthusiasm for dramatic performance itself. He describes *opsis* ('spectacle') by stating: 'Staging can be emotionally attractive, but is not a matter of art and not integral to poetry. The power of tragedy can be exercised without actors and without a performance. Staging belongs more to the scene-painter's art than to that of the poets'.[34] Elsewhere in the *Poetics*, Aristotle comments that tragedy 'produces its effect even without movement; its quality is apparent from a mere reading'.[35] Aristotle himself, being an ancient Macedonian who lived a generation or two after the great tragedians, probably read more tragedy than he ever watched. His perspective has undoubtedly contributed to a longstanding critical tendency to prefer analysing dramatic tragedy as literary text rather than as a performance, with Aristotle downplaying aspects of tragedy such as music and spectacle.

There is also another critical bias that is generated here by Aristotle, and one that is sometimes overlooked by those who memorize his tragic terminology. We only have a single book of the *Poetics*, and, although Aristotle declares that he is going to speak of comedy, he fails to do this in the surviving volume. In the *Rhetoric*, Aristotle says he has distinguished forms of the laughable in the *Poetics*, but this promised analysis is absent from the extant book.[36] The fact that Aristotle's treatise on comedy disappeared, whilst his ideas about tragedy became central to ideas about Western drama following the European rediscovery of the *Poetics* in the 1500s, meant that tragedy became widely seen as the top-notch mode for theatrical writing, and there has long been a sense that a successful playwright should write tragedy and be considered through a tragic prism.

Over time, performed tragedy became popular in both republican and imperial Rome, drawing on Greek examples, but also using elements from Rome's own performance traditions. The only complete tragedies to survive from this period are those of Seneca, and his gruesomely violent plays became an important model for playwrights in later European history. In England, the Shakespearean period saw a particular flourishing of staged plays labelled by theatre makers and publishers as tragedies, which showed the downfall of exalted figures; whilst in German drama of around 1800 there appeared another blossoming of plays by authors such as Goethe, Kleist, and Schiller that encouraged audiences in an age of political upheaval to attend to the suffering or death of various heroic individuals. Yet although playwrights repeatedly deployed varying tragic ideas, for many years after Plato and Aristotle the idea of tragedy had a more limited purchase in the realm of philosophical and abstract thinking. This situation changed towards the end of the eighteenth century, when German Idealist philosophers showed a fresh enthusiasm for the subject, prompted at least in part by the popularity of German translations of Shakespeare and by an awareness that neighbouring France had enjoyed a vogue for restaging Greek tragedies during the preceding century.[37] As Jonah M. Johnson puts it, philosophical debates about the tragic became 'inflected by the struggle of German intellectuals to foster a national character by means of a national theater', and such German theorizing influenced much thinking about tragedy during subsequent eras.[38]

One of the most significant of these thinkers was Hegel, who found that tragedy primarily resided in the contemplation of 'a conflict and its resolution'.[39] Hegel looked particularly at Sophocles' play *Antigone* and found that it demonstrated the clash of two equally valid principles, the values of the family (embodied by Antigone) clashing against the values of the city (embodied by Creon). As Hegel put it, *Antigone* is:

one of the most sublime and in every respect most excellent works of art of all time. Everything in this tragedy is logical; the public law of the state is set in conflict over against inner family love and duty to a brother; the woman, Antigone, has the family interest as her 'pathos', Creon, the man, has the welfare of the community as his.[40]

Hegel's influential idea was that out of this conflict might emerge a sense of higher justice and resolution. For him, tragedy focused not primarily upon a great tragic hero, but upon a confrontation of equally justified principles, values, or powers. In addition to these formal ideas, Hegel stated that drama 'must be regarded as the highest stage of poetry and of art generally', and within his discussion of drama he often described tragedy in particularly heightened terms (Sophocles' *Oedipus at Colonus*, for example, is, for Hegel, 'beautiful', 'most perfect', and 'eternally marvellous').[41] Thus, parts of Hegel's writing may have helped to contribute to a certain snobbery around tragedy, and a subsequent critical sense that it is perhaps most fitting to discuss celebrated modern dramatists such as Henrik Ibsen, Anton Chekhov, August Strindberg, Lorraine Hansberry, Sarah Kane, or Suzan-Lori Parks as creators of tragedy, even though they could equally well be classified as comic writers.

A generation after Hegel, Nietzsche rejected Hegel's account of Greek theatre as a site of logic and order, and sought to emphasize instead the violence and chaos of tragedy. Nietzsche famously contrasted the Apollonian drive (towards characteristics such as reason and individuality) with the Dionysiac drive (towards irrationality, drunkenness, and loss of self-control). Schopenhauer also reacted against earlier Idealist thinking, but continued to feel concerned with tragedy. He argued that 'Tragedy should be viewed, and is in fact recognized, as the pinnacle of literature', and described it as 'the highest of poetic achievements'. Schopenhauer can scarcely be considered the cheeriest of thinkers, valuing tragic art because 'the unspeakable pain, the misery of humanity, the triumph of wickedness, the scornful domination of chance, and the hopeless fall of the righteous and the innocent are brought before us here: for here we find a significant intimation as to the nature of the world and of existence'. He declared, 'in tragedy we see that, after a long struggle and much suffering, the noblest people eventually renounce forever the goals they had, up to that point, pursued so intensely [...] they all die, purified by suffering, i.e. after the will to live has already died out inside them'.[42] There are doubtless many undergraduates today who, having been compelled to complete a 3,000-word essay on tragedy, will recognize the sentiment. Still, the ideas of Nietzsche, and then subsequently those of Schopenhauer, became widely influential in the nineteenth century, and, as we shall see, affected the thinking of twentieth-century playwrights such as Yeats and Beckett.

However, although those German philosophers felt deeply influenced by dramatic texts such as *Antigone*, they tended to avoid considering tragedy primarily as theatre. Admittedly, Hegel did explore some theatrical aspects in his *Lectures on Aesthetics*, and Hölderlin also considered tragedy as a dramatic form, but in general those thinkers tended to concentrate on tragedy as a philosophical paradigm rather than as something that might have very much to do with the greasepaint, flats, and costumes of the playhouse.

In the meantime, although Shakespeare in Britain enjoyed a heightened reputation, as did a select group of playwrights in other national traditions, by the dawn of the nineteenth century tragedy had generally lost its dominant position. In very broad terms, as the twentieth century approached, the anglophone theatre saw a wide array of forms, from violent blood-and-thunder barnstormers to pantomimes, often designed to elicit strong feelings from an audience. Carolyn Williams asserts that, on the English stage during the Victorian era, 'Melodrama replaces tragedy', and those notably popular melodramatic plays depicted a world that generally resolved according to a Christian schema of poetic justice, devoid of the great clashes of principle that Hegel had found in tragedy, and lacking the Nietzschean battle between the Apollonian and Dionysiac.[43] Instead, virtue tended to be rewarded, and vice punished. The writer of melodrama often played the role of an orderly and organizing Abrahamic god, rebalancing the moral order of the theatrical universe, and ensuring that characters received their just deserts (honest heroines rescued and married, mustachioed malefactors apprehended and punished, etc.). One critic felt moved to comment on a performance by the actor Henry Irving that deviated from this model: 'Mr. Irving pictures a villain as so despicable a being that one feels it a personal injury at the close of the play that he is not killed, or left for execution'.[44]

Nonetheless, some popular melodrama did enter into a productive dialogue with earlier tragic models. Melodrama might resolve in satisfaction rather than sorrow, but in certain respects the precipitous fall of the melodramatic antihero recalls that of the older tragic hero. Furthermore, for many, the sense of the prevailing Christian balance of the universe was significantly undermined during the Victorian period. Publications such as Marx and Engels's *Manifesto of the Communist Party* (1848) and Darwin's *On the Origin of Species* (1859) encouraged renewed questioning of established social, natural, and moral structures. By the time that Queen Victoria died in 1901, the unavoidable cruelty of the Shakespearean and Greek theatres potentially spoke to the contemporary moment more appropriately than the neatly resolved world of melodrama.

In this context, during the early 1900s, a number of prominent anglophone theatre makers looked afresh at the tragedies of the Greeks and to various stripped-back versions of Shakespeare. The play that was so influential in defining Aristotle's ideas of tragedy, Sophocles' *Oedipus Rex*, was in fact banned from performance in England, Wales, and Scotland at the start of the twentieth century. In 1904, Great Britain's official censor, a member of the royal household called the Lord Chamberlain, refused permission for the actor-manager Herbert Beerbohm Tree to stage the piece in public. Bernard Shaw observed, 'The Lord Chamberlain prohibits one play by Sophocles because, like Hamlet, it mentions the subject of incest', and then Shaw wondered whether the censor should likewise 'suppress all the plays of Euripides because Euripides, like Ibsen, was a revolutionary Freethinker'.[45] For Shaw, Euripides thought independently of authority in a distinctly modern way by doubting long-held religious dogma, and Shaw noted other themes in age-old tragedies that might chime with the priorities of his own era.[46] When Shaw looked at Shakespearean drama, he observed that the modern producer of *King Lear* might also be liable for prosecution because Shakespeare's play contains 'perhaps the most appalling blasphemy that despair ever uttered'.[47] After all, in Shakespeare's play, the dead Cordelia appears immediately after Albany declares 'The gods defend her!' (V, iii, 252), and elsewhere Gloucester declares: 'As flies to wanton boys are we to th' gods:/ They kill us for their sport' (IV, i, 35–6). To some at least, such articulations of despair may have felt freshly appropriate at the start of a century that began with ominous portents including a stock-market crash (New York, 1901), the establishment of concentration camps by the British (during the Second Anglo-Boer war, 1899–1902), and the assassination of the American president (William McKinley, 1901).

J. Michael Walton describes how, with the arrival of the twentieth century:

> the great tragedians began to emerge from the vaults to which they had been consigned, their plays, or some of them, renewed and reinvigorated through translation. It was a far from painless process. In 1903 there were riots in the streets of Athens when Thomas Economou presented Aeschylus' *Oresteia* in modern rather than ancient Greek. Several people were killed.[48]

There followed various experiments to revive aspects of the tragic art by early twentieth-century theatre makers. Gordon Craig, for example, found inspiration in the tragedies of ancient Greece. As Christopher Innes puts it:

> the creative process of the Greek theater, in which Aeschylus had instructed the chorus in their dances as well as the protagonists in how they should deliver their lines, and in

which the dramatist and director were the same person, was precisely what Craig aimed at [...] it was also the principles of an architectural, multipurpose setting (as distinct from specific or two-dimensional scenes), symbolic acting, simplicity.[49]

The Royal Court Theatre in London, under the management of Harley Granville Barker, initiated a serious attempt to revive the essence of Greek tragedy, and to demonstrate the contemporary political relevance of such drama. Granville Barker befriended Gilbert Murray, the Regius Chair of Greek at Oxford from 1908, who published translations of Euripides that were taken up by numerous theatre groups, including working-class organizations. Murray's plays found a home at the Royal Court, where the management allowed for the kind of experiment rarely facilitated elsewhere. Edith Hall points to what was probably the first performance of a modern-language translation of Euripides' *Trojan Woman*, which took place at the Royal Court in 1905 in a translation by Murray. As Hall puts it, this production was written:

in order to protest against the concentration camps in which the British had incarcerated Boer women and children during the terrible war in South Africa. Murray was convinced that Euripides had written the play to protest against the very recent Athenian massacre of many of the male inhabitants of the rebellious island of Melos [...] Murray's 'pacifist' interpretation has been widely embraced, and led to a whole series of performances during and after World War I.[50]

Likewise, it is possible to see Murray's version of *Medea* (1907) as one of the first of the suffragette plays that would include Elizabeth Robins's *Votes for Women* (1907) and Cicely Hamilton and Christopher St John's *How the Vote Was Won* (1909). Murray's rendering of plays including *Hippolytus*, *The Bacchae*, and *Medea* all appeared at the Royal Court in the years before the First World War. One critic, W.H. Salter, writing between 1909 and 1910, asked of Euripides:

Does he not, with Prof. Gilbert Murray for interpreter, find his natural place on our stage by the side of our newest and brainiest dramatists? Is he not familiar to all Fleet Street as the 'Greek Ibsen', the 'Attic Shaw'? Are not his plays an inexhaustible mine of tags for the Feminist and other workers for Great Causes?[51]

As Bernard Shaw observed, Murray 'has not merely translated Euripides – many fools have done that [...] he has reincarnated Euripides and made him a living poet in our midst'.[52] In 1908, Murray's translation of the *Bacchae* was staged by William Poel, providing the first production of Euripides' tragedy on an English stage, with Poel also being the director who had worked to rid Shakespearean drama of many nineteenth-century accretions.[53] Poel attempted to restore Shakespeare's work to something like the conditions of its original performance by experimenting with features such as the boy actor in female roles and with a bare platform stage. Under Poel, the visual excess of Shakespearean tragedy was pruned back to something altogether starker, and potentially more likely to focus audience attention upon the aural rather than the spectacular.

In this context, some playwrights now attempted to create versions of tragedy that might rely upon the importance of verse speaking. Although the British censor had refused *Oedipus Rex* a licence for public performance in 1904, by November 1910 he had granted a licence for a translation of the play by Gilbert Murray. W.B. Yeats then published an adaptation of Sophocles' *Oedipus Rex* in 1928, and subtitled it '*A Version for the Modern Stage*', before publishing a version of *Oedipus at Colonus* in 1934. The influence of Greek and Shakespearean tragedy could be noted in an assortment of Yeats's own original verse plays, which feature chanted lyrics, masks, and the downfall of figures from history and legend.

Meanwhile, T.S. Eliot produced a range of contemporary verse plays inspired by Greek tragedies, including *The Family Reunion* (1939, based on Aeschylus's *Oresteia*), *The Cocktail Party* (1949, based on Euripides' *Alcestis*), and *The Elder Statesman* (1958, based on Sophocles' *Oedipus at Colonus*).

Other playwrights, however, created original dramas that emulated tragic models but avoided the heightened verse-speaking and heroic gods or ghosts of Yeats (indeed, Eliot's theatre moved further in this opposite direction as his career progressed: the verse and classical allusions become increasingly difficult to discern in his later plays). After all, by the start of the twentieth century, Freud had argued that modern tragedy was really a drama of the interior human mind. In *The Interpretation of Dreams* (1899), Freud decried the idea that tragedy would teach a contemporary spectator 'submission to the divine will and realization of his own impotence'.[54] Instead, Freud declared that the tragedy of Oedipus had a different message: Sophocles' play revealed the incestuous desire that all men might share. For Freud, Oedipus's destiny:

> moves us only because it might have been ours – because the oracle laid the same curse upon us before our birth as upon him. It is the fate of all of us, perhaps, to direct our first sexual impulse towards our mother and our first hatred and our first murderous wish against our father. Our dreams convince us that it is so. King Oedipus, who slew his father Laïus and married his mother Jocasta, merely shows us the fulfilment of our own childhood wishes.[55]

For Freud, *Hamlet* showed the story of the title character whose uncle has actually achieved what Hamlet had himself wanted to do: kill young Hamlet's father and sleep with the protagonist's mother. Claudius shows the prince of Denmark 'the repressed wishes of his [Hamlet's] own childhood realized. Thus the loathing which should drive him on to revenge is replaced in him by self-reproaches, by scruples of conscience, which remind him that he himself is literally no better than the sinner whom he is to punish'.[56]

We might well question some of Freud's assertions about tragic drama (isn't Oedipus the one person who certainly doesn't have an Oedipus complex? His first sexual impulse could scarcely have been aimed towards the mother he didn't know). But Freud nonetheless helped usher in an era of tragedy associated with the interior life of the mind, and with the everyday life of ordinary people. Not everyone owns a royal house, but everyone possesses their own psychological domain, and, as Emily Dickinson reminds us, one need not be a chamber to be haunted. In the playhouse, Freud's thinking dovetailed with that of Henrik Ibsen, whose dramatic work was first promoted during the late 1800s and early 1900s in the English-speaking world by figures including William Archer and Bernard Shaw. In a celebrated essay of 1891, *The Quintessence of Ibsenism*, Shaw praised Ibsen, in terms that sound proto-Brechtian, for 'writing realistic prose plays of modern life [...] no more tragedy for the sake of tears'.[57]

Henrik Ibsen recycled the Aristotelian principles of plot construction in order to create modern dramas that might portray the miseries of ordinary people: the suicide of unhappily married Hedda Gabler, the drowning of Little Eyolf, the domestic claustrophobia of Nora Helmer, or the inherited syphilis of Oswald Alving. On Ibsen's stage, life was sometimes unbearably cruel, and fate bore little relationship to a character's moral behaviour or to notions of Christian redemption. Ibsen thus helped to usher tragedy away from the heightened realm of the royal palace, and into the provincial living room, where audiences could hear the everyday words and observe the day-to-day worries of the middle class. In the fourth century BCE, Aristotle had famously declared that the protagonist of theatrical tragedy 'is a personage enjoying renown and prosperity, such as Oedipus, Thyestes, and eminent persons from families of that kind', and A.C. Bradley maintained in *Shakespearean Tragedy* (1904) that: 'A Shakespearean tragedy as so far considered may be called a story of exceptional calamity leading to the death of a man in high estate'.[58] But Ibsen created plays that focused on the tragedy of the Norwegian bourgeoisie. His art avoids the realm of princes, warriors, and nobles, and focuses on the personal dilemmas and mental turmoil of doctors, journalists, and bank managers.

The dialogue of Ibsen's best-known drama, which depicts psychologically recognizable states, is far removed from the stylized chanting of Sophocles and the heightened verse of Shakespeare. After all, as Bradley put it, a tale 'of a man slowly worn to death by disease, poverty, little cares, sordid vices, petty persecutions, however piteous or dreadful it might be, would not be tragic in the Shakespearean sense'.[59] So how can those contrasting realms of Shakespeare, Sophocles, and Ibsen be considered under the same critical mantle? In 1949, Arthur Miller addressed this issue as he premiered his play *Death of a Salesman*, a work full of realistic dialogue that follows Ibsen in depicting a middle-class man who commits suicide after facing various personal and professional disappointments. In the *New York Times*, the leading critic Brooks Atkinson published a review of *Death of a Salesman* under the headline 'Arthur Miller's Tragedy of an Ordinary Man', arguing that 'everybody recognizes in his tragic play things they know are poignantly true', pointing to the setting that was 'tragic in mood', praising the lead character because 'his tragedy is great', and hailing the 'tragic acting'.[60] The *Washington Post* agreed that, in this play set amidst modern Brooklyn, Miller had 'rediscovered the secret of the all-but-lost art of tragedy', and the London *Times* labelled the play 'immediately tragic'.[61] At the same time as receiving such acclaim, Miller published his own feelings about tragic drama, placing a piece in the *New York Times* with the title 'Tragedy and the Common Man'. In this essay, Miller explained that people of the modern world, with their scepticism and science, may be disinclined to believe in heroes, but that tragedy is scarcely an anachronism. Miller interpreted the 'tragic flaw' as the hero's unwillingness to accept circumstances as they are, something that can equally well apply to characters in the present day as in the past. The individual's fight against fate, environment, and circumstances provided the opportunity to democratize tragedy. As Miller put it, 'such a process is not beyond the common man'.[62]

Miller's ideas found an echo in Raymond Williams's famous study of 1966, *Modern Tragedy*. Williams took aim at George Steiner, and argued that the literary and vernacular uses of the term 'tragedy' may exist in close alignment. It might be, noted Williams, 'very common for men trained in what is now the academic tradition to be impatient and even contemptuous of what they regard as loose and vulgar uses of "tragedy" in ordinary speech and in newspapers'.[63] Yet, as Williams contended, tragic thinking could in fact be expressed in day-to-day speech, and:

> In an ordinary life, spanning the middle years of the twentieth century, I have known what I believe to be tragedy, in several forms [...] I have known tragedy in a man driven back to silence, in an unregarded working life. In his ordinary and private death, I saw a terrifying loss of connection between men, and even between father and son.[64]

A key part of *Death of a Salesman* revolves around a similar loss of connection between father and sons, and there is an obvious overlap between Arthur Miller's advocacy of the tragedy of the 'common man' and Raymond Williams's idea of the tragedy of 'ordinary life'. Yet both men largely concentrated upon carefully crafted writing. Miller is best known as a dialogue-heavy playwright, and Williams's *Modern Tragedy* stays within the realm of literary theory. Nonetheless, Williams and Miller made an important point about challenging the antidemocratic way in which, ever since Aristotle, writers and critics had often tended to view 'ordinary' and 'common' lives as being removed from the domain of true tragedy.[65]

Williams and Miller believed that notions of tragedy retained significance and valency in the modern era, and the current volume takes its cue from Williams, who identified modern tragedy as that specific form that, after a period of evolution, first became generally apparent from the second half of the nineteenth century, with the arrival of figures such as Ibsen, Strindberg, and Chekhov. But, as we have seen, a number of critics and theatre makers declared that the tragic form, with its backward-looking focus upon concepts such as God and the tragic hero, simply could not be retrofitted to make it suitable for this era. For example, as we have noted, Walter Benjamin saw tragedy as redundant and felt that, instead, a modern 'epic' theatre now 'consists in producing not empathy but astonishment. In a word: instead of identifying with the protagonist, the audience should learn to feel astonished at the circumstances under which he functions'.[66] Here Benjamin echoed the thinking of his friend, Bertolt Brecht, who felt that accepting Aristotelian notions of tragedy was to fall into a kind of fatalism, to believe that things could not be changed, and to subscribe to a set of 'natural laws' that provided a shared reality and understanding.

Yet Brecht himself repeatedly created drama that emulated pre-existing tragic models. His play *Mother Courage*, for example, revolves around a mother who loses her children to an unavoidable wartime fate. Brecht himself anxiously realized that he had created an heroic figure of universal motherhood, and he complained that when the 'bourgeois press' looked at *Mother Courage*, critics tended 'to talk about a Niobe-like tragedy'.[67] Indeed, after first completing the play, he repeatedly revised the main character to make her less sympathetic.[68] But if Aristotelian catharsis might make audiences supine, Brecht nonetheless wished to use certain tragic themes and ideas in order to raise political awareness. As Chapter 2 of this book will demonstrate, he therefore retooled earlier tragic narratives as a response to contemporary events including the Spanish Civil War and the Second World War.

Brecht's use of tragedy offers an instructive comparison with other theatre makers. Peter Szondi, in his *Theory of the Modern Drama* (published in German in 1956, English in 1987), highlights the significance of the Belgian playwright Maurice Maeterlinck, who wrote his best-known works in the final years of the nineteenth century and the first years of the twentieth. Szondi argues that Maeterlinck's work is dominated by death, but that:

> no action brings on death, no one is responsible for it. From the dramatic point of view, this means that the category 'action' is replaced by 'situation'. The genre Maeterlinck created should, in fact, bear this name, because the essential in each of these plays does not reside in the action. They are, therefore, no longer 'Dramas' – as long as the Greek word is understood in this sense. It is this distinction that lies being the rather paradoxical term *drame statique*, which Maeterlinck coined for his work.[69]

Szondi identifies the key idea of Maeterlinck's drama: 'Maeterlinck's decision to dramatize the human situation as he saw it led him to present his characters as silent, suffering objects in the hands of death. He did this within a form that, until then, had known only speaking, active subjects'.[70] Patrick McGuinness identifies Maeterlinck's affinity with Samuel Beckett in that respect, describing how:

> Like Beckett's, Maeterlinck's characters are *tied* to the place in which we find them, the 'en attendant' of theatre, whose dual function is to promise change, while binding them to the boredom and uncertainty of the interim. Boredom, anguish, extemporization, and 'second degree dialogue' are all responses to time as it emerges through the magnifying lens of the wait.[71]

Lehmann points out that Maeterlinck identified a *tragique quotidien* ('tragedy of the everyday'), which Maeterlinck felt to be the only decent modern form of tragedy. As Maeterlinck puts it: 'There is a tragic element in the life of every day that is far more real, far more penetrating, far more akin to the true self that is in us than the tragedy that lies in great adventure'.[72]

This everyday kind of tragedy, then, has little to do with Aristotle. Instead, as Lehmann writes, 'Death becomes the driving force behind tragic experience, but in a way wholly different than in classical tragedy: namely through its omnipresence'. In the *tragique quotidien*, 'Characters inhabit a threatening world with death always close at hand. This entails a certain "fatalism", the motif of keeping silent, which points to the unspeakable abyss that the self represents'.[73] In such tragedy, death is always nearby; characters inhabit a world of threat and danger; and, according to Lehmann, the tragic experience 'does not refer to experience which is supposed of the tragic hero, but rather to the experience of those who witness – or, as the case may be, "live through"– the tragic process as spectators and observers'.[74] Lehmann's formulation helps point us towards understanding why the work of a playwright like Samuel Beckett might be considered tragic, as well as suggesting why modern tragedy might be considered primarily in terms of theatre and performance, rather than through, say, the novel or some other textually transmitted form.

Other critics have emphasized that tragedy only really deserves to retain its purchase as a theatrical concept in the twentieth and twenty-first centuries if it is opened up for consideration beyond the realm of the white European men whose dramatic and philosophical writings have long dominated the tragic discussion. Pelagia Goulimari argues that 'the strife of the decolonizing process and its postcolonial aftermath were the context for a return of tragedy', pointing out that prominent theorists of tragedy such as Eagleton and Steiner have been 'strangely blind' to this fact.[75] Indeed, Ato Quayson, in his important study *Tragedy and Colonial Literature*, points out that Williams and Steiner are 'unified by an almost complete disinterest in what takes place outside the borders of Euro-America', and argues that the absence of references to literature from former colonies is 'difficult to explain in Terry Eagleton's [study of tragedy] *Sweet Violence*, which was published in 2005'.[76] Yet as David Scott contends, the anticolonial moment may be particularly ripe for tragic thinking. Ridding a people of colonial domination provided 'another moment of violent collision of opposing forces (colonialism and nationalism) in which horizons of expectation and idioms and frameworks of experience were often tragically at odds with each other'.[77] In the final chapter of this book, then, we will look at how tragic thinking may connect with the work of postcolonial theatre makers in the Caribbean and in Nigeria.

In our contemporary world, even if we open the realm of tragic theatre to a range of differing viewpoints, it can nonetheless feel like, at best, a bizarre luxury to spend time cogitating upon the realm of the tragic. In the era of disastrous climate change, when the food scarcity and malnutrition that afflict millions of people every day are continually worsened by environmental degradation, for audiences and readers to spend time worrying about tragic theatre might appear a costly distraction from more pressing issues. Yet the themes and ideas of tragedy may nonetheless speak to, and illuminate, today's dire situation. In the early 1970s, the biologist Joseph Meeker followed a path once trodden by Aristotle in moving from the academic study of biology to the study of literature, and wrote a book, *The Comedy of Survival*, which anticipates later ecocriticism, and which helps expose an entire system of thought that has led to the current moment of environmental emergency. Although Meeker's volume tended to be overlooked when first published, he proved impressively prescient. '[N]either tragedy nor ecological crisis could have developed as they have without the interweaving of a few basic ideas which have attained in the Western tradition an importance far greater than they carry in other cultures', he observed, 'the assumption that nature exists for the benefit of mankind, the belief that human morality transcends natural limitations, and humanism's insistence upon the supreme importance of the individual personality'.[78] As Meeker puts it, the environmental calamity that has emerged and worsened since the second half of the twentieth century owes a debt to

Western anthropocentrism, which holds mankind above the natural world. This tradition can be traced back to the kind of hero seen in the ancient Greek theatre. For Meeker, tragedy is associated with human agency and the destructive actions that represent heroic freedom, with human life given meaning by the struggles in which such individuals engage and in the learning that results. Meeker felt particularly moved by the passage from Sophocles' *Antigone* about human supremacy over nature, which includes the lines: 'A cunning fellow is man. His contrivances/ make him master of beasts of the field'.[79] As Meeker points out, 'It is no accident that a rhapsody extolling man's conquests over nature appears at a crucial point in Greek tragic drama, for man's spiritual elevation above his natural environment is an essential tragic assertion'.[80] Such a view of mankind's dominance over nature certainly continues in later tragedies. The planetary scale of a global environmental calamity is arguably beyond the scope of Shakespearean tragedy, with its focus on the fall of an exceptional person, and Simon Estok even argues that 'the height of individualism in Shakespeare's tragedies marks also a high point of anthropocentric thinking and desires for environmental control'.[81] Indeed, much tragedy tends to affirm the status of the natural world as subordinate to that of humanity. *Macbeth*, for example, shows some remarkably porous boundaries between the human and non-human, but it would take a rather unusual interpretation, or some very unorthodox directorial decisions, to lead a spectator into feeling more concerned with the trees of Birnam Wood rather than the fate of the titular character.

In modern drama, however, it is possible to find examples of playwrights breaking down the division between human and nature in a way that encourages questioning of the subordination of the non-human. For example, when W.B. Yeats scripted his short drama *At the Hawk's Well* (1917), he nominally used the Japanese Noh tradition but also drew on features common to Attic drama and described feeling inspired by 'the tragic image that has stirred my imagination'.[82] Here Yeats created a title character who has an integral relationship with whether or not water will flow in the vicinity, and who confuses the other characters about whether she is human, avian, or supernatural.[83] She also appears different in substance and size to the human characters around her. An old man sees her as 'that girl there' who is likely to 'murder or betray'.[84] A legendary Irish hero refers to her as 'That woman', but also says to her, 'Grey bird, you shall be perched upon my wrist', and wonders 'why does she not cry out as the hawk cries?'[85] The title character in Yeats's tragic play, then, is both a seductive woman *and* a bird of prey. Furthermore, Natalie Crohn Schmitt points out that Yeats also 'chose for the role a male dancer who was not disguised as a female. Is the hawk embodied in the girl one being or two? Is it male or female, human or animal, natural or supernatural? It seems that this figure takes many forms; and that the distinction between one and many does not apply to it'.[86] From the twenty-first-century perspective, when public discourse increasingly displays alertness to non-binary gender identities and awareness of human interconnectedness with the natural world, aspects of Yeats's tragic vision can appear somewhat premonitory.

As I have been attempting to indicate in this introduction, tragedy has proven a sufficiently capacious term to incorporate a very broad array of philosophical ideas and theatrical texts. According to Emily Wilson, one of the problems with studying tragedy is that 'it can involve a lack of cultural or political specificity, and a neglect of the historical facts about a very discontinuous tradition'.[87] The three chapters of this book *Forms of Drama: Modern Tragedy* will therefore focus upon particular case studies from indicative moments in the history of the form in order to show how tragedy might be reappraised in theatrical writing at different points in time according to varying precepts and principles. The first chapter is motivated by the urgency of our current situation in the Anthropocene era, and so focuses upon John Millington Synge's work *Riders to the Sea*, a 1904 play that influenced W.B. Yeats's thinking about tragedy and which Daniel J. Casey calls 'Synge's nature-elegy'.[88] This chapter shows how a sensitive environmental awareness might be expressed through tragic drama. After all, as Joy Kennedy puts it, in this work the sea is absolutely central: it 'functions as both the provider for the family and its potential destroyer', and Eagleton describes the ocean in this play as one of modernity's 'substitutes for the gods'.[89] In Synge's work, then, we may find a modern drama that incorporates an environmental ethos into its notion of tragedy, with Synge's heightened awareness of nature giving his playwriting a particular resonance in our own era, as well as, at times, drawing Synge's theatre towards the philosophical realm of the Nietzschean. Ultimately, *Riders to the Sea* goes beyond simply being a narrative about the heroic individual, and instead becomes one in which the individual is subsumed into a broader story about community, location, and the natural world.

The two ensuing chapters will highlight theatre makers who adapted aspects of *Riders to the Sea* in order to achieve very different results than Synge. The second part of this book will take a detailed look at Brecht's reworking of Synge's drama in the 1937 play *Señora Carrar's Rifles*. This chapter will examine Brecht's script in the light of his broader ideas about tragedy, noting that Brecht felt earlier tragedies tended to leave their audiences emotionally stimulated but stunted in terms of political understanding and response. Brecht evidently borrowed from Synge in creating *Señora Carrar's Rifles*, and was happy to derive ideas from earlier tragic dramas: elsewhere, he proved to be one of many twentieth-century theatre makers who used the story of *Antigone* in order to tell a modernized tale about the individual battling against the state. But some of Brecht's ideas of tragedy emerged in an era when Beckettian theatre appeared to move tragedy towards a *tragique quotidien*. By contrast with Brecht's theatre-making, which was informed by Hegel and Marx, Beckett worked in a different, Schopenhauerian, tradition of tragic thinking. Nonetheless, Beckett and Brecht's approaches to tragedy did not prove entirely irreconcilable, with Brecht himself attempting to create a version of Beckett's *Waiting for Godot*.

Finally, the third chapter of this book will examine theatre makers whose ideas were, at least in part, motivated by utilizing an understanding of the tragic narrative of *Riders to the Sea* within postcolonial contexts. Derek Walcott's 1954 play *The Sea at Dauphin* echoes aspects of Synge's play but is set the work among a fishing community in the village of Dauphin on Saint Lucia, and deploys a set of ideas that are distinct from those of Western tragedy. Meanwhile J.P. Clark's 1961 play *Song of a Goat* is also by a writer who knew *Riders to the Sea*, but who seeks to explore ideas of death, loss, and sacrifice among the Ijaw fishing community of the Niger Delta. The chapter examines how tragedy might be reformulated in order to address the experiences and concerns of non-white authors and audiences, and asks whether a comparison of African and Caribbean drama with older European theatrical examples necessarily positions postcolonial drama in a secondary and subordinate position. To put it bluntly, in an era when technology makes us increasingly aware of global exploitation, and of injustices suffered on a routine basis by minorities even in very rich countries, how might we approach a canonical body of work that skews towards a white male view of traumatic subjects such as misogyny, rape, and xenophobia? The book concludes by discussing the work of Nigerian playwright Greg Mbajiorgu, whose *Wake Up Everyone* (2011) combines the environmental awareness of Synge, the political urgency of Brecht, and like Walcott and Clark suggests a postcolonial theatrical approach that may point, however tentatively, towards a view of tragedy that allows for contemporary perspectives that are dissenting and contradictory.

1

From 1904: Synge and the nature elegy

On 25 April 1904, spectators watched the first performance of Synge's one-act play *Riders to the Sea*, at the Molesworth Hall in Dublin. The drama was performed by the Irish National Theatre Society, a venture that had been spearheaded under varying titles by W.B. Yeats and Lady Augusta Gregory since 1899, and which, later in 1904, would move into a permanent home and subsequently become well known as the Abbey Theatre. Yet Synge's *Riders to the Sea* scarcely proved an instant success. The actor George Roberts observed that the play 'did not win much praise in Dublin on its first performance. Some of the audience [members] were horrified at the sight of a corpse on the stage, a few of them left the hall while the performance was going on'.[1] At first, newspaper critics also tended to dislike the piece, with the reviewer for the *Irish Independent* commenting that the piece was 'too dreadfully doleful'.[2] The *United Irishman* also wished for something altogether jollier, declaring that 'we need sunshine badly'.[3] Meanwhile, the *Irish Times* deemed the play 'repulsive'.[4]

Nonetheless, since that time, critics have widely recognized the play as a masterpiece of modern tragic theatre. As Philip G. Hill put it in 1991: '*Riders to the Sea* is frequently cited as the best one-act play ever written. Certainly it is a remarkable achievement in capturing the tragic mood in so brief a time'.[5]

For Robert Welch, writing in 1999, Synge's play is a 'perfectly constructed tragedy' and demonstrates 'tragic writing at its finest'.[6] More recently, in 2021, Hélène Lecossois describes *Riders to the Sea* as depicting 'tragic but irrevocable loss'.[7]

Aristotle wrote the defining treatise on tragedy, but we know next to nothing from that short text about anything remotely sad ever having happened to him. By contrast, the context of Synge's writing is often connected with, and perhaps overshadowed by, the unfortunate fate of the playwright. Synge had been suffering from Hodgkin's disease since the 1890s, and would die at the age of just thirty-seven, almost exactly five years after the premiere of *Riders to the Sea*. Synge's life and work, then, often tend to be read with the Marlovian sense that 'Cut is the branch that might have grown full straight'.[8]

Quite aside from Synge's biography, the narrative of *Riders to the Sea* is replete with plenty of sorrow and grief. The play is set on one of the remote Aran islands off the west coast of Ireland. The action revolves around a matriarch, Maurya, who is, at the start of the play, mourning for her missing son Michael, whom she fears drowned. Her worry is well founded, as she has already lost five other sons and her husband to the ocean. She also feels deeply anxious about her final son, Bartley, who wishes to set off for sea. Bartley insists on leaving to sell his horse at a fair on the mainland, and she withholds her blessing from him as he departs. Maurya's daughters then unwrap a parcel of clothing recovered from the ocean, which confirms that her other son, Michael, is indeed dead. Maurya herself sees a disturbing vision of Michael riding on a horse behind the one being guided by Bartley. The play concludes with the arrival of Maurya's neighbours who inform the mother that her final living son, Bartley, has indeed died in the ocean, having been knocked into the waves by the horse he led to market. Bartley's corpse is brought onto the stage, and Maurya grieves over body, reflecting fatalistically that 'there isn't anything more the sea can do to me [...] No man at all can be living for ever, and we must be satisfied'.[9]

By the time that Synge's *Riders to the Sea* was first performed in Dublin during 1904, the theatrical possibilities of Greek tragedy had begun to attract attention from elsewhere in the burgeoning Irish national theatre movement. During a reading tour of 1903, W.B. Yeats spotted *Oedipus Rex* being performed at Notre Dame University in the United States. He commented, 'The play was forbidden by the English censorship on the ground of its immorality; Oedipus commits incest; but if a Catholic university could perform it in America my own theatre could perform it in Ireland. Ireland has no censorship, and a successful performance might make her proud of her freedom'.[10]

Unsurprisingly, then, the first person to describe Synge's *Riders to the Sea* in terms of theatrical tragedy was W.B. Yeats, who read the piece at an early stage and reportedly exclaimed aloud that Synge 'is like Æschylus' and declared Aeschylus 'The man who is like Synge'.[11] For sure, *Riders to the Sea* manifests certain formal similarities to Aeschylean drama. The deaths of Attic tragedy generally occur offstage, with bodies then displayed on an *ekkyklêma*. In Aeschylus's *Agamemnon*, for instance, Clytemnestra kills her husband Agamemnon offstage, and his bloodied corpse is then revealed on the wheeled platform as she announces her rule of the city. Likewise, in *Riders to the Sea*, audiences do not see the death of Bartley, which takes place offstage, but, at the culmination of the play, his body is brought onto the stage as Maurya laments her loss.

Synge himself certainly knew about Attic tragedy, and his diary for 29 April 1892 observes that he spent his time absorbed in *Stories from the Greek Tragedians*.[12] This 1880 prose volume by Alfred J. Church contains tales of characters including Medea, Antigone, and Agamemnon. Synge's diary records that he finished the book on 6 May 1892, and certain passages in Church's volume resonate with Synge's subsequent writing.[13] For example, Church repeatedly refers to the devouring sea 'covered with bodies of men and wrecks' and 'full [...] of bodies of dead men'.[14] In *Riders to the Sea* the women express concern for Michael's 'clean burial', just as in Church's book there is a recurring worry about those who 'lie unburied'.[15] Furthermore, the Antigone figure depicted by Church gives a lament that prefigures some of Synge's dialogue. In Church's volume, Antigone declares:

> But think now what sorrows are come upon our house. For our father perished miserably, having first put out his own eyes; and our mother hanged herself with her own hands; and our two brothers fell in one day, each by the other's spear; and now we two only are left.[16]

In Synge's *Riders to the Sea*, Maurya similarly recounts the family deaths:

> I've had a husband, and a husband's father, and six sons in this house [...] but they're gone now, the lot of them ... There were Stephen, and Shawn, were lost in the great wind [...] There was Sheamus and his father, and his own father again, were lost in a dark night, and not a stick or sign was seen of them when the sun went up. There was Patch after was drowned out of a curagh [...] may He [God] have mercy on my soul, Nora, and on the soul of everyone is left [...].[17]

When audiences first watched Synge's *Riders to the Sea*, the play's atmosphere of death and mourning certainly struck some observers as tragic. After Synge's work premiered, one spectator, Joseph Holloway, reflected, 'The audience was so deeply moved by the tragic gloom of the terrible scene on which the curtains close in, that it could not applaud'.[18] The first London performance of the work, at the Royalty Theatre on 26 March 1904, prompted the *Manchester Guardian* to declare that this was 'a little tragedy of great beauty and power [...] one was constantly struck and moved, as one is when witnessing actual tragic calamity, by its quietude where tragedy in books is noisiest'. The work was that of a 'tragic genius', who produced a 'final tragic cadence', and who 'has written a play steeped in the august and quiet sadness of Greek tragedy'.[19] Likewise, when the play appeared in the United States, the *New York Times* hailed the work as 'complete tragedy'.[20]

Later critics have repeatedly labelled Synge's play as tragic by noting comparisons with Attic drama.[21] However, Greek tragic theatre was filled with gods, semi-gods, and royalty. The tragedy of *Medea* revolves around the daughter of the king of Colchis who is also the granddaughter of the sun god, Helios. The story is scarcely focused on the messenger or the nurse. Indeed, Medea herself ends that play in the god-like position of manning a flying chariot drawn by winged serpents. A similar dynamic applies in the early modern period. The tragedy of *Hamlet* is that of the prince of Denmark: it is not the tragedy of Osric or of the gravedigger. Likewise, when the philosopher-poet Friedrich Hölderlin scripted his unfinished tragedy *The Death of Empedocles* towards the end of the 1700s he created a protagonist who reaches dizzying heights of spiritual and intellectual achievement, and who views the rest of humanity from a position of magnificent elevation. Before the end of the play Empedocles addresses the sun to say:

> O beauteous sun! human beings did not
> Instruct me, it was my holy heart compelled me
> Immortally to love immortals, drove me
> To you [...] thus I, belonging to
> The best of souls, to you, was happy to bestow all
> That I possessed on mortals.[22]

Tragedy thus became associated with 'towering, exceptional personages'. As George Steiner puts it, 'Social status, a representative role in the community being, in ancient Greece, in Elizabethan-Jacobean England, in the Europe of the *ancien régime*, a virtually self-evident, unexamined correlative'.[23]

However, by the start of the twentieth century, as *Riders to the Sea* shows, it was not axiomatic that high social status necessarily indicated the kind of 'self awareness', 'introspective dramatization', and 'literacy of consciousness' that Steiner highlights as being associated with tragic protagonists.[24] In Europe, after the revolutions of the nineteenth century, in the wake of Ibsen, and during an age of growing enfranchisement, dramatists positioned characters from less exalted social positions as the protagonists of tragic theatre.

If Synge's *Riders to the Sea* includes calamity, that calamity is of a repeated and almost workaday nature. By the end of the play, seven members of the same relatively anonymous family (Synge never gives them a surname) have been killed by the sea, so the individual death of Bartley can hardly be considered 'exceptional'. The figures of the play are peasants eking out a subsistence existence, far removed from the centres of cultural and political power. In addition, these are peasants who evidently engage with the everyday realm of modern commerce: the family initially finds it difficult to tell if the garments found in the sea belong to the missing son Michael because that clothing is made of material which comes from 'great rolls [...] in the shops of Galway', and so could belong to anyone.[25]

As Steiner puts it, with a nod to Arthur Miller: 'Even salesmen undergo heart-rending deaths'. But Steiner observed that *more* was needed in order for an artistic work to achieve tragic stature, writing that tragedy requires 'loftiness, complexity, concentration of speech' which was likely socially hierarchic: 'Wherever literature attempts to resuscitate high tragedy, in Ibsen's *Brand*, in the orientalising formalities of Yeats [...] the instrument is that of verse. This is not how common men and women express themselves. Tragic discourse characterizes the few'.[26] Yet in Synge's work there is an embrace of the way that 'common men and women express themselves'. As Barry McCrea puts it, 'Hiberno-English, in one sense, was now being used as though it were the language of Racine'.[27] Synge himself scarcely came from peasant stock; he was a well-travelled member of the Anglo-Irish ascendancy and *au fait* with the Parisian avant-garde. But he also journeyed through rural Ireland, jotting down the striking words and phrases that he heard there. As he admitted, when thinking about how he wrote *In the Shadow of the Glen*, 'I got more aid than any learning could have given me, from a chink in the floor of the old Wicklow house where I was staying, that let me hear what was being said by the servant girls in the kitchen'.[28] Grammatical features such as the immediate perfective in Synge's work ('The young priest is after bringing them') can sound idiosyncratic to non-Irish ears, but such phrasing maps onto Irish-language usage (*tar éis* = after).[29] Consequently, as Declan Kiberd has observed, Synge's 'language is a heightened version of natural peasant speech. This heightening is achieved by emphasizing those aspects of peasant dialect which have their source in Gaelic speech and syntax'.[30]

In the characters of Synge's *Riders to the Sea*, then, we find an exaggerated version of the pronunciation, vocabulary, and syntax used by the peasantry in the west of Ireland. This language is scarcely the voice of prestige and influence. Let us take one specific example, the final instruction that Bartley gives to the women of the play before his death, which can be quite difficult for audiences to understand:

> If the west wind holds with the last bit of the moon let you and Nora get up weed enough for another cock for the kelp.[31]

That line situates the play's action in a very particular socio-economic setting. Here, the impoverished, female members of this community must work outdoors, dependent on the weather at dawn, to collect seaweed or 'kelp' in order to create a stacked heap or 'cock'. For Bartley, the material on this 'cock' might then be dried during any suitable weather remaining in the month. The material could be burned down and then traded, providing what was then the principal cash product of the Aran islands, used in products such as glass, soap, and gunpowder.[32]

Synge could, of course, have scripted the line about kelp in the kind of language that I have just used. But instead he put this phrase in a heightened version of Aran dialect, with its distinctive vocabulary and word order, and so ensured that the theatre event became defamiliarized for middle-class patrons. If someone from the islands might feel bewildered by the codes of mainland society, Synge's drama ensured that those from relatively well-heeled backgrounds who watched this play in Dublin – and especially those who subsequently watched in English towns or the east-coast cities of the United States – would potentially encounter similar moments of befuddlement. Despite the assertions of Synge's early readers such as Maurice Bourgeois, who tended to see the playwright as apolitical, in later years, scholars of Synge have increasingly analysed the political implications of Synge's work, and there is undoubtedly an anticolonial message in staging a play about the distinctive language and culture of the rural Irish at a time when Ireland was still ruled from London and the country uneasily incorporated into the British state.[33]

Additionally, as Synge's dialogue shows, there might be a particular kind of aesthetic beauty in this enhanced variety of peasant speech. Synge's characters speak a version of English that resembles that spoken in the west of Ireland, but such language could scarcely be considered anybody's everyday talk. As Barry McCrea puts it, the idiom of Synge's play:

> cleaves more closely to Gaelic syntax than the English actually spoken in Ireland ever did. It is not always clear whether the characters are really speaking the local form of English or whether they are 'really' supposed to be speaking an Irish that is being translated for us. [...] Not only is his dialect something he himself never spoke naturally, it was a language no one ever spoke in real life either.[34]

Steiner identified that tragic language might be associated with 'loftiness, complexity, concentration of speech'.[35] Synge's synthetic Irish speech certainly delivers lofty thoughts about fate, and expresses deeply felt and complex emotions with remarkable concentration. But Synge, by associating this language so closely with the hardship of the peasant experience, showed that tragedy might not simply be associated with the misfortunes of the privileged and the princely. For Synge, modern tragedy might thrive in a peasant cottage just as much as in a royal court.

An indication of how Synge's use of Irish-inflected English might articulate the ideas associated with classical tragedy can be found perhaps most clearly in the fatalistic lines spoken by Maurya which conclude the play:

> Michael has a clean burial in the far north, by the grace of the Almighty God. Bartley will have a fine coffin out of the white boards, and a deep grave surely ....What more can we want than that? ... No man at all can be living for ever, and we must be satisfied.[36]

Critics have tended to connect this sentiment with that of Attic tragedy.[37] There are, certainly, distinct parallels between Sophocles' drama and that of Synge, perhaps most notably when we compare Maurya's final line ('we must be satisfied') with the concluding words of Sophocles' *Oedipus at Colonus*, spoken by the chorus, which recommend submission to the gods:

> ἀλλ' ἀποπαύετε μηδ' ἐπὶ πλείω
> θρῆνον ἐγείρετε·
> πάντως γὰρ ἔχει τάδε κύρος.[38]

These lines are rendered in Francis Storr's 1912 English translation as: 'Wail no more, let sorrow rest,/ All is ordered for the best'.[39] Sophocles' lines strike a similar note of acceptance and human powerlessness to those closing lines of Synge, and some translators have certainly added Syngean language to subsequent translations of Sophocles' play.[40]

However, although later critics and translators have connected Synge with Sophocles, the influence is not necessarily a direct one. Indeed, that apparently Sophoclean phrase in

Riders to the Sea, 'No man at all can be living for ever, and we must be satisfied', owes a debt to a 1902 letter written in Irish by Martin McDonough, a boy from the Aran Islands who had befriended Synge. McDonough's letter includes the line:

> it fell out that the wife of my brother Sean died, and she was buried the last Sunday of the month of December and look! that it is a sad story to tell, but if it is itself, we must be satisfied because nobody can be living forever.[41]

As Declan Kiberd puts it:

> Synge might seem to have taken his own final sentence from some related proverb in the west of Ireland. No such proverb exists, however, and the source can only be Martin's letter. Far from composing an idiom unrepresentative of peasant speech, Synge has here translated into English the simple idiom of an island boy for the climactic scene of his most tense play. In lines such as these, he allowed the islanders to speak directly for themselves.[42]

Hence, in that line from Synge's work we may find an example of how, in the twentieth century, as Arthur Miller asserts, 'the common man is as apt a subject for tragedy in its highest sense as kings were'.[43] Synge's line chimes with the closing of *Oedipus at Colonus*, and may owe something of its incorporation into the script's conclusion to Synge's reading of tragic drama, but was also directly inspired by the circumstances, grief, and language of everyday peasant life. Hence, in Synge's *Riders to the Sea* we find a tragedy woven from the experiences of those who spend their time, '*kneading cake*', spinning '*at the wheel*', or ensuring that 'the sheep aren't jumping in on the rye'.[44]

The English dramatist John Masefield was deeply influenced by Synge's tragic thinking. According to Masefield, he and Synge were such good friends that for a time they met 'almost daily', and Synge shared early playwriting and photographs of Aran with Masefield.[45] Masefield then sought to create his own theatrical tragedy, feeling that 'Tragedy at its best is a vision of the heart of life. The heart of life can only be laid bare in the agony and exultation of dreadful acts'.[46] Masefield therefore wrote the 1908 play *The Tragedy of Nan*, and in doing so, sought to echo Synge's work. Hence, *The Tragedy of Nan* concludes with a suicidal drowning, and is set in a rural area, the countryside of South West England, which the author declared was 'among a people and in a place well known to me'.[47] Masefield's play also relies on dialect in order to convey meaning, with the dialogue consisting of phrases such as: "Er said 'er'd tell you to onst. It was a accidenk'.[48]

D.H. Lawrence also followed Synge, agreeing that the ordinary life of working people could prove fertile territory for tragedy. But whereas John Masefield set *The Tragedy of Nan* in 1810, Lawrence felt that the lives of his contemporaries made an apt subject for the tragic form. Synge's *Riders to the Sea* so impressed Lawrence that he pronounced it 'the genuinest bit of dramatic tragedy, English, since Shakspere'.[49] Lawrence then sought to write his own version of the story in a play called *The Widowing of Mrs Holroyd* (published 1914), relocating the action to a twentieth-century coal-mining community in the English East Midlands, and using the strong regional dialect of that area. Lawrence's characters make statements such as: 'I shonna. I'll settle him. Shut thy claver. He'll non come anigh thee'.[50] Thus, whereas the men of *Riders to the Sea* repeatedly return to the ocean, even after disaster, the men of Lawrence's *The Widowing of Mrs Holroyd* return to the collieries, and in each case the dramatic action revolves in gendered terms around the womenfolk of these communities who, in the wake of calamity, are left to survive and to mourn. Lawrence's play is sufficiently similar to Synge's that when Lawrence's script first received a professional British premiere in 1926, the *Manchester Guardian* noted that 'The play stops with a lamentation in which Holroyd's mother bemoans her many slaughtered sons. It is a "keening" like the close of "Riders to the Sea"'.[51]

In relocating Synge's work in this way, Lawrence showed
that the tragic story need not only work in the kind of arena
that Terry Eagleton defines as a 'pre-modern margin', but in
a twentieth-century miner's cottage, where characters such
as an electrician and a middle-class manager are surrounded
by details such as a '*chintz-backed sofa*', a '*glass-knobbed
painted dresser*', and a view onto the '*colliery rail*'.[52] As
Lawrence put it when describing his mining dramas, the
particularities of twentieth-century life meant that earlier
notions of tragic situations needed to be extended. He
declared, 'we have added another tragic possibility to the
list: the Strike situation', and 'Granted that men are men
still, Labour v. Capitalism is a tragic struggle'. However,
in such scenarios, it was important that tragic characters
remained interesting because of their human capacities
rather than becoming viewed as 'bits, parts, machine-
sections'. As Lawrence put it, thinking in Hegelian terms,
'Tragedy is not disaster. It is a disaster when a cart-wheel
goes over a frog, but it is not tragedy. Tragedy is the working
out of some immediate passional problem within the soul of
man [...] There must be a supreme *struggle*'.[53] For Lawrence,
the tragic impulse could be incorporated into the modern
spaces of contemporary life, but only if considered in terms
of personal dilemmas, antagonisms, and confrontation.

By allowing everyday griefs and individual sorrows to
displace atypical brutality and exceptional heroes, Lawrence
and Synge had moved in the direction of Maurice Maeterlinck,
the nineteenth-century dramatist who, as we have noted,
advocated a *tragique quotidien*. For Maeterlinck, theatrical
tragedy appeared generally caught in a kind of time warp.
Tragic playwrights tended to imagine that audiences would
'delight in witnessing the very same acts that brought joy to
the hearts of the barbarians, with whom murder, outrage, and
treachery were matters of daily occurrence'.[54] But Maeterlinck
argued that, for modern spectators, 'it is far away from
bloodshed, battle-cry, and sword-thrust that the lives of most
of us flow on', and he observed that 'There is a tragic element in

the life of every day that is far more real, far more penetrating, far more akin to the true self that is in us than the tragedy that lies in great adventure'.[55] For Maeterlinck, then, *Hamlet* might provide a superior tragic model to *Othello* because Othello is all jealous passion, which is not necessarily the condition in which we live our truest lives, whereas Hamlet at least has time to deliberate, to avoid taking action, and to consider his own existential condition. Maeterlinck himself declared that he went to the theatre not hoping to see such violence, such 'life of bygone days', but 'hoping that the beauty, the grandeur and the earnestness of my humble day by day existence would, for one instant, be revealed to me, that I would be shown the I know not what presence, power or God that is ever with me in my room'.[56] Tragic theatre, for Maeterlinck, might be found in stillness rather than in 'the violence of the anecdote', and so the writer of modern tragedy might be encouraged to emulate the painter who realizes:

> that the solemn voice of men and things, the voice that issues forth so timidly and hesitatingly, cannot be heard amidst the idle uproar of acts of violence. And therefore will he place on his canvas a house lost in the heart of the country, an open door at the end of a passage, a face or hands at rest, and by these simple images will he add to our consciousness of life, which is a possession that it is no longer possible to lose.[57]

But Maeterlinck's observations raise the question of whether such modern tragedy of the everyday is truly contiguous with classical models of tragedy. Certainly, one person who cited those earlier models in order to profess scepticism about whether Synge's drama really qualified as tragic was James Joyce.

Joyce was in his early twenties, and Synge in his early thirties, when they met in Paris during spring 1903. The two literary rivals then enjoyed a series of combustible lunches on the rue Saint-André-des-Arts, with the two men clashing over the merit of Synge's then recently completed *Riders to the Sea*.[58] Joyce initially expressed his antipathy towards the play, and if this dislike was somewhat motivated by professional jealousy, he nonetheless dressed it up as a theoretically justified position based on notions of tragedy. Joyce first learned about *Riders to the Sea* in January 1903, from an impressed Yeats, and Joyce had seen a copy for himself by March. Joyce then wrote to his brother:

> Yeats told me it was quite Greek: and I suppose Synge will be boomed now by the Irish Theatre – the plays are all in one act. Synge gave me the MS of 'Riders to the Sea' and I have read it: it is a play of Aran in peasant dialect. I am glad to say that ever since I read it I have been riddling it mentally till it has [not] a sound spot. It is tragic about all the men that are drowned in the islands: but thanks be to God Synge isn't an Aristotelian.[59]

Joyce proved only too happy to repeat this condemnation of *Riders to the Sea* to Synge himself. Synge protested, 'It's a good play, as good as any one-act play can be', but Joyce maintained that Synge had only produced a 'dwarf drama'.[60]

Joyce was rapidly developing his own aesthetic ideas during this time, and Synge found his compatriot a stickler for formal Aristotelian definitions. Joyce offers a parallel here with his fictional character of Stephen Dedalus, who, in *A Portrait of the Artist as a Young Man*, attempts to define tragedy:

> A girl got into a hansom a few days ago [...] She was on her way to meet her mother whom she had not seen for many years. At the corner of a street the shaft of a lorry shivered the window of the hansom in the shape of a star. A long fine needle of the shivered glass pierced her heart. She died on the instant. The reporter called it a tragic death. It is not. It is remote from terror and pity according to the terms of my definitions.[61]

In real life, Joyce offered a similar condemnation of Synge's work from an Aristotelian perspective. Yet, despite Joyce's initial feelings about *Riders to the Sea*, as his sibling points out, 'the rhythm of certain phrases had stuck in my brother's memory'. James Joyce 'already knew Maurya's final speeches almost by heart – and he repeated them with such a keen sense of their beauty that it must have tempered his strictures'.[62]

Consequently, when Joyce lived in Trieste during 1909, he spent time translating Synge's play into Italian, with the assistance of the lawyer Nicolò Vidacovich. As with Lawrence's *The Widowing of Mrs Holroyd*, Joyce's translation showed how Synge's text might move beyond the geographical borders of Ireland. Joyce and Vidacovich, for example, worked at the correct word for a horse's 'halter' by pondering French and Italian alternatives, Italianized several character names, and considered an Italian version of Maurya's pivotal benediction 'God speed you'.[63] After Synge's death in 1909, Joyce abortively tried to get the translation produced by Alfredo Sainati's Italian Grand Guignol Company. Later, Joyce even collaborated with the actor Claud Sykes to form a theatre company which would produce *Riders to the Sea* in Swiss cities. Joyce's efforts therefore prefigured the way that, as we shall see, theatre makers such as Bertolt Brecht and Derek Walcott would take Synge's tragedy, and relocate it into very different geographical and temporal settings.

Riders to the Sea also affected James Joyce's own prose writing. Anne Fogarty has identified echoes of *Riders to the Sea* in Joyce's short story collection *Dubliners* (1914), and she suggests that his novel *Ulysses* (1922) takes a cue from Joyce's Aristotelian thinking about *Riders to the Sea* by likewise reworking 'classical sources in a modern context'.[64] But perhaps the final pages of Joyce's final novel *Finnegans Wake* (1939) come closest to the conclusion of *Riders to the Sea*. Synge's script ends with female characters swaying and keening, whilst the mother of the household, Maurya, reflects on the fact that all of her male offspring have been lost to the waves. As she sprinkles holy water on the dead body of her last son, she calls to mind the acoustic landscape of the ocean:

> I'll have no call now to be up crying and praying when the wind breaks from the south, and you can hear the surf is in the east, and the surf is in the west, making a great stir with the two noises, and they hitting one on the other.[65]

At the end of *Finnegans Wake*, the character 'ALP' concludes the work with another monologue that emphasizes both the soundscape of the sea and the omnipresence of death.[66] As Philip Kitcher writes of the last eight pages of Joyce's novel, here the reader finds 'the perspective of the retrospective appraisal, the woman who sees the end and looks backward, seeking to come to terms with the course of her life'.[67] In the very final paragraph of *Finnegans Wake*, ALP echoes one of the recurring phrases of *Riders to the Sea*: whereas Synge's characters repeatedly worry about a dead family member literally being 'washed up', ALP declares 'I sink I'd die down over his feet, humbly dumbly, only to washup'.[68]

Joyce, then, borrowed ideas from Synge's tragic drama to help create an entirely different literary mode, adapting performed drama into the realm of the avant-garde novel. Such a shifting of forms, and a willingness to question the porousness of various genres, is a distinct feature of tragic thinking from the late 1700s, since when the label 'tragic' has been appended to cultural items including ballets, orchestral compositions, and films. Some of the formal promiscuity of tragic thinking in the twentieth century is shown by the fact that *Riders to the Sea* would be made into a film by 1935, and repeatedly adapted into musical versions by figures including Henri Rabaud, Marga Richter, Eduard Pütz, and Ralph Vaughan Williams.[69]

Nonetheless, this volume largely maintains a focus on theatrical tragedy, in part because of the Greek origins of the term, and in part because, as Hans-Thies Lehmann has emphasized, 'tragic experience' may describe a process of

specifically theatrical witnessing.[70] Bert Cardullo asks of
Synge's play, 'what do we learn from *Riders*? Not to wish for
the death of our son? That excessive fear or anxiety breeds
superstitiousness? But didn't we know all this before? Of
course we did'.[71] For Cardullo, what Synge instead had
succeeded in creating is 'tragedy of an elemental order that we
have not seen since the Greeks'.[72] According to this way of
thinking, Synge created a drama in which spoken words take
on a rhythmic, quasi-musical quality; where the sensory labour
of spinning and preparing bread takes place before spectators;
and where the rituals of grief are enacted in real time before
an audience. This drama is experiential, and defies replication
in a textual medium such as the novel. As a result, it can feel
that the classroom or library study of Synge's script fails to
encompass adequately the playwright's art. In his performed
tragedy, Synge gives domestic drudgery and rural labour a
kind of dignity by paying close attention to all of those daily
rhythms and conflicts, which a live audience is encouraged
to share. *Riders to the Sea* asks spectators to sit down and
attend to this life, and, through that communal witnessing, to
appreciate that these lives might be as full of poetic utterance,
deep sorrow, and unavoidable suffering as any of the lives
which had long been considered by thinkers and theatre
makers as more suitable subjects for tragedy.

Joyce's appropriations of *Riders to the Sea*, then, may
provoke questions about the generic borders of tragedy. But
those appropriations also highlight certain ideas in Synge's
script that give the tragedy a continuing relevance today. In
Joyce's *Finnegans Wake*, ALP echoes the words of *Riders to
the Sea*, and here the human character is not set above nature,
rather, the human character merges into nature. ALP herself
seems, at various points, to be a human woman, but at other
points she appears to be a river, and at the end of the novel she
is flowing out to meet her 'cold mad feary father', the sea.[73]
This melding of the individual into the world of nature is also
something that features prominently in Synge's *Riders to the
Sea*. Before he scripted the play, Synge wrote about his real-life

visits to the Aran Islands, recording his encounters with the people, language, and customs of the three isles. At one point in his travel journals, eventually published as *The Aran Islands* in 1907, Synge wrote about a funeral, during which hail began to fall and thunder to rumble. Synge wrote: 'one is forced to believe in a sympathy between man and nature'.[74] He continued:

> The grief of the keen is no personal complaint for the death of one woman over eighty years, but seems to contain the whole passionate rage that lurks somewhere in every native of the island. In this cry of pain the inner consciousness of the people seems to lay itself bare for an instant, and to reveal the mood of beings who feel their isolation in the face of a universe that wars on them with winds and seas.[75]

As Rónán McDonald has put it, when looking at this passage, although a single old woman has died:

> the attitude of the people extends beyond individual mourning to find some putatively universal resonance. This mysterious sympathy is a prelude for a moment of sheer *anagnorisis* which is more communal than individual [...] Synge himself seems to endorse this notion that the keening might move the process of mourning away from the individual and into a communal realm in which mankind might share feelings of loss with the surrounding natural world.[76]

When Synge came to write *Riders to the Sea*, he again looked at the keen in order to express and contain what McDonald calls 'communal rage' and 'communal catharsis'.[77]

In *Riders to the Sea*, when Maurya's last son dies, Maurya begins to keen. But she is not mourning one isolated individual. Although it is ostensibly her son Bartley whom she grieves, and it is his body that lies on the stage, the keen goes beyond the individual and expresses a sorrow for her dead men who are 'all together this time'.[78] Maurya pines:

> I'll have no call now to be up crying and praying when the wind breaks from the south, and you can hear the surf is in the east, and the surf is in the west, making a great stir with the two noises, and they hitting one on the other.[79]

In this lamentation, Maurya's sons remain relatively helpless, but the sea itself has agency. It is the sea that 'can do [things] to me', it is the sea that can spend its time 'making a great stir with the two noises', and it is the sea whose two parts can be 'hitting one on the other'. In Joy Kennedy's ecocritical reading of the play, she writes of Maurya, 'it should be noted that she and the other women remain passive to the ocean's force'.[80] Kennedy may slightly overstate that passivity: after all, Maurya does actively try to stop Bartley from going to the sea. But at times the natural world simply takes more decisive actions than any of the human characters. For example, the concluding death of the play is caused not by human agency but by an animal. A gray pony knocks Bartley into the surf and kills him, and the fact that nature causes the death was one of the features of the play that made the young Joyce feel that *Riders to the Sea* did not really qualify as a tragedy.

Kennedy points out that this natural realm is thoroughly distinct from the ecosystem described by British nature poets such as Coleridge and Wordsworth, whose reflections scarcely risk dissolving the individual human into the environment, and instead maintain a focus on the discrete individual's lone pilgrimages through particular landscapes. By contrast, for Synge, the Aran Islands manifested power because, as he put it, the 'people make no distinction between the natural and the supernatural'.[81] In this way, Synge's thinking about nature and the environment connects him with the tragic ideas of Friedrich Nietzsche.[82] In tragedy, Nietzsche saw a divide between the Dionysiac chorus and the Apollonian dialogue spoken by key protagonists. During the course of a tragedy, the hero tends to realize the frailty of his distinct identity, and become drawn towards the Dionysiac. There is a feeling of release as individualism is destroyed and 'primal one-ness' is restored. In his 1872 book *The Birth of Tragedy*, Nietzsche asserted:

> Under the spell of the Dionysian it is not only the bond between man and man which is re-established: nature in its estranged, hostile, or subjugated forms also celebrates its reconciliation with its prodigal son, man. The earth voluntarily gives up its spoils while the predators of cliffs and desert approach meekly. The chariot of Dionysus overflows with flowers and wreaths: beneath its yoke tread the panther and the tiger [...] now the animals speak and the earth gives forth milk and honey.[83]

This aspect of Nietzsche's thinking has led some critics to find in his work a strong parallel with the environmentalism that has emerged since the 1970s. Max Hallman expresses this idea in his 1991 article 'Nietzsche's Environmental Ethics', and he has been followed by scholars like Greg Garrad, who argues, 'Nietzsche, like deep ecologists, seeks a biocentric perspective'.[84] Similarly, Daniel R. White and Gert Hellerich identify in Nietzsche 'a good indication of what we now think of as an "ecological" sensibility'.[85] They point particularly to Nietzsche's early piece, 'Homer's Contest', where he says:

> If we speak of *humanity*, it is on the basic assumption that it should be that which *separates* man from nature and is his mark of distinction. But in reality there is no such separation: 'natural' characteristics and those called specifically 'human' have grown together inextricably. Man, at the finest height of his powers, is all nature and carries nature's uncanny dual character in himself.[86]

As Martin Drenthen puts it, 'Much of Nietzsche's philosophy can be seen as an attempt to come up with an account of nature that explains how all aspects of human nature are just elements of an all-embracing nature'.[87] After all, one biographical incident that remains relatively well known about Nietzsche is the instance of sympathy he showed for the natural world in 1899, when he saw a carthorse being whipped by its owner and felt so affected by the cruelty that he ran to the animal, embraced it, and then collapsed to the ground, in a moment that signalled the start of his permanent mental breakdown.[88]

In his thinking about tragedy, Nietzsche sought to identify a form that exceeded the bounds of human selfhood. In *The Birth of Tragedy* Nietzsche expressed the idea that individuality was simply an illusion and urged 'the fundamental knowledge of the unity of all that exists, the consideration of individuation as the original cause of evil, art as the joyful hope that the spell of individuation is to be broken, as the presentiment of a restored unity'.[89] As Paul Hammond contends, this means that:

the boundaries of the self are blurred, and neither we nor the protagonist can truly say what is self and what is not-self [...] Antigone is repeatedly seen as her father's child, not simply as herself. Tragedy asks, 'Who acts?', and again, 'Who speaks?' Characters begin to sound like other characters.[90]

In *The Birth of Tragedy*, Nietzsche emphasizes how aesthetic experiences provide a union with the natural world that might transcend the individual. As Nietzsche observes when describing the Dionysian: 'nature in its estranged, hostile, or subjugated forms also celebrates its reconciliation with its prodigal son, man'.[91] Indeed, during recent years, some biologists have moved to speak in distinctly Nietzschean terms, writing not of the singular human, but of the 'collective property of the human-associated microbiota'.[92]

If Nietzsche's thinking about the tragic had sought to assert a biocentric perspective that went beyond the discrete individual, shifting tragedy away from the remarkable heroes of Sophocles and Shakespeare, the same tendency could be noted in Synge. In his *Autobiography*, Synge writes about his teenage appreciation for nature:

To wander as I did for years through the dawn of the night with every nerve stiff and strained with expectation gives one a singular acquaintance with the essences of the world. The obscure noises of the owls and rabbits, the heavy scent of the hemlock and the flowers of the elder, the silent flight of the moths I was in search of gave me a passionate and receptive mood.[93]

As Seán Hewitt puts it, Synge commenced a 'nuanced exploration of ecological relationships' in which 'The techniques and principles of modern science are applied by the modern writer to suggest the potential of attaining a unity with nature'.[94] At times in Synge's nature writings, according to Hewitt, we find 'the idea that a landscape can provide a connection to something beyond itself, and that a person standing in that landscape can become part of a cosmic system'.[95]

Pre-twentieth-century tragedy had often appeared to tell 'a story of exceptional calamity leading to the death of a man in high estate'.[96] But by the time Synge came to write *Riders to the Sea*, he created a drama in which nature is the figure that propels events. In its personality, the sea begins to echo and absorb something of the temperament of Maurya, the character who also seeks to nurture and protect the men of the island but who feels responsible for destroying at least one of them. It is Maurya, after all, who physically places water on the onstage body at the end of the play. Additionally, the natural world is constantly making its presence felt through the expressions and descriptions spoken by the characters, and at one point, when a gust of wind blows the door open, the natural world threatens to intrude physically amongst the human characters. It is also the sea that carries the dead away: Maurya describes the dead Michael 'floating that way to the far north, and no one to keen him but the black hags that do be flying on the sea'.[97] Hewitt notes that Michael 'is left without *human* keeners' but that the 'black hags' provide 'a direct translation from the Irish for cormorant, *cailleach dhubh*', a phrase which adds 'a sense of the supernatural for the English-speaking audience'.[98] The personality of the sea is also expressed through features such as the fishing nets that are one of the first things mentioned as being situated onstage, and which indicate both threat of entrapment and death, and the possibility of sustenance and travel. As Kennedy puts it, the play's props 'reveal the connections, both physical and spiritual, between the characters and land, as well as the ecological interplay between them'.[99] After all, Synge himself had observed of the items that he found on Aran, such as fishing nets and oil skins, that 'they seem to exist as a natural link between the people and the world that is around them'.[100] When he looked at the cowskins, all ready to be made into pampooties (the rawhide shoes worn on the island), Synge reflected that 'Every article on these islands has an almost personal character'.[101] Modern tragedy may therefore demonstrate a shift from environment as condition of life – in, say, Ibsen – and environment as part of a dramatized interaction. In Ibsen's famous play, Nora may feel like a toy or marionette in the doll's house that has been constructed around her, but in Synge's work the characters are aware that the surrounding sea has its own interactive place in the drama, something that potentially gives *Riders to the Sea* a renewed purchase in our own era of well-publicized feedback loops between humankind and deforestation, humankind and pollution of the oceans, or humankind and warming of the climate.

Of course, Nietzsche scarcely maintained a consistent view on the individual throughout his life: by contrast with the parts of *The Birth of Tragedy* highlighted above, at other points he declared his belief that the 'sovereign individual' had emerged.[102] Ralph Acampora has noted that Nietzsche's 'high humanism' is aristocratic and individualistic, and so cannot really be considered the sort of 'biospheric egalitarianism' of today's ecologists.[103] Likewise, the narrative of Synge's *Riders to the Sea* does maintain a focus on its human protagonists. The feelings and actions of Maurya and her family remain at the heart of the drama. But the way in which Synge's tragic art showed the human individual interacting with, or at times even merging into, the natural world, helped point the way forward for one of his influential friends who was strongly influenced by Nietzschean ideas, W.B. Yeats.

In his essay 'The Tragic Theatre' (1910), W.B. Yeats defined tragedy as something that transcended a focus on the individual human character. By the time he wrote this piece, Yeats was himself grieving for Synge, who died in the spring of 1909, and Yeats's idiosyncratic essay is in some respects an attempt to comprehend the meaning and significance of death. Yeats thus opens his essay on 'The Tragic Theatre' by discussing Synge's work, arguing that in Syngean tragedy the audience would be 'carried beyond time and persons to where passion, living through its thousand purgatorial years, as in the wink of an eye, becomes wisdom'.[104] If a focus on individuated character might provide the base material for comedy, Yeats wanted tragic art to transcend this. As he put it in his essay:

> in mainly tragic art one distinguishes devices to exclude or lessen character, to diminish the power of that daily mood, to cheat or blind its too clear perception. If the real world is not altogether rejected, it is but touched here and there, and into the places we have left empty we summon rhythm, balance, pattern, images that remind us of vast passions, the vagueness of past times, all the chimeras that haunt the edge of trance.[105]

Otto Bohlmann analyses Yeats's essay 'The Tragic Theatre' by pointing out that, for Yeats:

> By providing 'the contemplation of things vaster than the individual', tragedy renders man 'as one' with nature. Through Dionysian 'intoxication', the 'drowner of dykes', we transcend the *anima hominis* ['soul of man'] and soar beyond the limits of 'character'.[106]

'The Tragic Theatre' repeatedly looks back to the kind of watery landscape that Synge had depicted in *Riders to the Sea*, with Yeats describing tragic art as that in which the individual rationality of Apollo breaks down in favour of the Dionysiac 'drowning and breaking of the dykes', 'an art of the flood', where 'We feel our minds expand convulsively or spread out slowly like some moon-brightened image-crowded sea'.[107]

Furthermore, Yeats's subsequent attempts at writing tragic drama repeatedly focus upon such moments when the borders of the individual human break down and merge with the broader natural world. The dramas that Yeats published in 1921 as *Four Plays for Dancers* have been considered in terms of their tragic qualities by thinkers including Maeve Good and Hans-Thies Lehmann, with those plays incorporating a number of conventionally tragic elements from the Attic world, including masks and chanted verses.[108] As Christopher Morash points out, Yeats was writing for stages that 'were simply too small for choric dancing', but Yeats nonetheless 'develops what we might think of as a "choric function" performed by a small group of musicians'.[109] In the best known of these dramas, Yeats's 1916 play, *At the Hawk's Well*, the characters describe natural features of the landscape as having their own agency. The wind is described as 'stupid', the shadows 'dance upon the desolate mountain', the water in the fountain plays a game of hide and seek with the characters, and the branches of the trees even appear to shout aloud.[110] Furthermore, the title character morphs, changes, and interacts with the natural world in a profound way. The character of Cuchulain, an aristocratic warrior from the mythological past, addresses the guardian of the well as 'bird, woman, or witch'.[111] As Sylvia Ellis has emphasized, the actor who originally played the part of the guardian readied himself for the role by spending 'hours outside the hawk aviary in London zoo meditating on the movements of the birds'.[112] Yeats may not have sanctioned this actorly preparation, but he had surely established a fictional figure for whom the contrast between the individual and the collective had become blurred, and who could scarcely be considered fully individuated.

Furthermore, *At the Hawk's Well* begins with an image of environmental catastrophe, as the chorus opens the action by describing:

A well long choked up and dry
And boughs long stripped by the wind [...]
The mountain-side grows dark;
The withered leaves of the hazel
Half choke the dry bed of the well.[113]

As Natalie Crohn Schmitt puts it, 'throughout the play the hazel trees and the well serve as a silent warning [...] Cuchulain has come to a place of death'.[114] In this environment, the chorus wonders about the value of human life, asking of one man, 'What were his life done soon! Would he lose by that or win?'[115] Here the fate of the human characters is closely connected with that of the surrounding natural environment.

A comparable environmental message can be found elsewhere in Yeats's *Four Plays for Dancers*. For example, in his 1917 work *The Dreaming of the Bones* the characters again merge into the natural world. One figure describes herself and her lover as 'but shadows/ Hovering between a thorn-tree and a stone', whilst the chorus labels elements of the natural world with human emotions: 'Birds cry, they cry their loneliness./ Even the sunlight can be lonely here'.[116] Once more, though, if the characters are blending into their surroundings, the characters worry about the despoilment and degradation of that environment. A young Irish rebel decries deforestation, observing that 'English robbers/ Cut down the trees or set them on fire'.[117] He also criticizes the destructive techniques of food production, admonishing the 'drinking cattle' for having 'Fouled' the water supply.[118] He even laments the pollution of modern industry, noting that, if not for the arrival of the English, the country would have remained 'beautiful' because 'we have neither coal, nor iron ore,/ To make us wealthy and corrupt the air'.[119]

By the time that Yeats published his dance play *The Only Jealousy of Emer* in 1919, one of the main characters engages in a physical fight against the sea. This battle leaves the figure of Cuchulain apparently dead at the start of the play. When Yeats rewrote a prose version of the piece, as the play *Fighting the Waves* (1930), his initial stage directions are clear that Cuchulain '*supposes the waves to be his enemies*', and that '*The waves may be represented by other dancers*'.[120] In performance, then, the human and the non-human are blurred, and Cuchulain is physically and mentally absorbed by the sea. When Yeats described the mask used for the prose version he wrote, 'I am deeply grateful for a mask with the silver glitter of a fish, for a dance with an eddy like that of water, for music that suggests, not the vagueness, but the rhythm of the sea'.[121]

As Joseph Meeker points out, in classical tragedy there exists a deeply anti-environmental message. Meeker declares, 'man's spiritual elevation above his natural environment is an essential tragic assertion'.[122] However, at the start of the twentieth century, Synge and Yeats developed ideas of the tragic, which for them coincided with Nietzschean thinking, that undermined notions of human separation and elevation. Of course, there is some contradiction to be found here, as Yeats and Synge continued to show considerable interest in particular tragic humans, and the merging of nature and humanity is not necessarily an ecological issue for these writers. In Synge's *Riders to the Sea*, the body of Bartley ultimately lies in the midst of all, just as in *The Only Jealousy of Emer* the washed-up body of Cuchulain is placed centre stage.

Nonetheless, in Yeats's *Four Plays for Dancers* and in Synge's *Riders to the Sea* there emerges a profound attentiveness to the natural environment, and that environment repeatedly subsumes the characters. The tragedy becomes not entirely that of discrete figures within a landscape, but that of figures *and* their landscape. Here, then, we may find a nascent version of the kind of environmentally aware writings that Ursula K. Heise praises for rethinking the relationship between the individual and the global.[123] Synge, and later Yeats, depict doom-laden stories that nonetheless draw attention to the natural forces shaping human destiny, with those stories emphasizing the interdependence of humankind and nature.

Steiner contends that this broad narrative of tragedy has been repeatedly played out in different forms throughout human history. He writes:

> The Judeo-Christian and Pauline fable of Adamic disobedience and inherited guilt has darkened the human prospect virtually to our day. It has modulated with intriguing ease into secular and profane models. Marx's 1844 manuscripts postulate a stage [...] dooming our species to the treadmill of labor and class conflict [...] Freud's legend, equally evasive as to time and place, is one of original parricide [...] In each of these foundational narratives, the Adamic blueprint, however secularized, is unmistakable. Some distant, dread crime or error, the tension between these two categories being crucial to tragedy (*hamartia*), has sentenced man to the ever-renewed cycle of frustration, of individual and collective self-destruction.[124]

In recent years, this 'Adamic blueprint' looks more familiar in an ecological context. For example, in Yuval Noah Harari's bestselling book, *Sapiens: A Brief History of Humankind* (published in Hebrew in 2011, English in 2014), we find the following assessment of the impact of human beings upon the planet:

> Ecological disasters occurred on almost every one of the thousands of islands that pepper the Atlantic Ocean, Indian Ocean, Arctic Ocean and Mediterranean Sea. Archaeologists have discovered on even the tiniest islands evidence of the existence of birds, insects and snails that lived there for countless generations, only to vanish when the first human farmers arrived [...] The First Wave Extinction, which accompanied the spread of the foragers, was followed by

the Second Wave Extinction, which accompanied the spread
of the farmers, and gives us an important perspective on the
Third Wave Extinction, which industrial activity is causing
today.[125]

Today's readers may be increasingly aware that this is their
narrative of original sin. Even an individual who personally
leads an extremely abstemious lifestyle comes from a line of
ancestors who have been responsible for wave upon wave
of environmental destruction, from the clearing of ancient
woodlands to the burning of fossil fuel. To have been born
may be sinful, not because we inherit the *felix culpa* of Adam,
but because, even in the process of our arrival, we inherit and
develop a carbon footprint that accelerates the destruction
of many aspects of natural world. To be aware of modern
environmental despoilment is to ask, as the tragic protagonist
must, to what extent should I struggle in order to escape my
fate, and to what extent do I bear responsibility?

Seeing a play by John Millington Synge is, of course,
unlikely to help matters in a directly practical way. In fact,
staging drama usually involves a considerable carbon cost, not
least in terms of lighting and regulating the temperature of an
auditorium, constructing the stage sets, and transporting an
audience to the venue. As Drew Milne has highlighted, 'The
sites of contemporary tragic performance have been forced to
reflect on their own role in environmental sustainability'. But
Milne then adds, 'Ecological crisis turns out to have been an
implicit condition of the cultural history of modern tragedy,
and in ways now made newly explicit', and what Synge does,
in *Riders to the Sea*, is to develop a sense of tragedy that
emphasizes how humanity and nature might be profoundly
interlinked, something that feels freshly relevant in our current
age.[126] Ultimately, Synge demonstrates that there may be ways
of talking about the calamity of our situation in terms of the
collective and communal rather than in those terms of the
individual and the self which tend to be preferred by liberal
democracy and consumer capitalism.

However, given the seriousness of today's ecocidal situation, we may feel compelled to wonder whether it is sufficient simply to have our emotions roused about such topics. If theatre audiences merely feel emotions and then return home 'purged' of those feelings, might there be something wasteful or improper about the dramatic art form? As we shall see, for some who have considered modern tragedy, solely experiencing some kind of catharsis was quite beside the point. Theatre in the modern age, if it was to have any value and meaning at all, had to assume a form that encouraged its spectators to rethink established ideas, to change, and to take action.

Enter Brecht.

2

From 1937: Brecht and political engagement

In 1934, Francisco Franco was promoted to major general in Spain, and then helped lead the brutal suppression of an uprising of Asturian miners. By July 1936 he had joined a group of generals who launched a coup against the elected left-wing government, and by October 1936 he was installed as head of state. His seizure of power precipitated a civil war that lasted for more than three years, with Franco ruling over a government which was effectively a military dictatorship. He drew inspiration and support from Hitler and Mussolini, with Franco's supporters rallying in the style of the Nazis.[1]

In appalled reaction, the Bulgarian film director Slatan Dudow asked Bertolt Brecht for a short drama that might be staged by Franco's opponents, and Brecht responded by scripting a one-act play. This piece was Brecht's first attempt to create a script that had a contemporary political crisis as its starting point, and he largely completed the piece in the first half of 1937.[2]

At this politically febrile time, cultural figures across the West worried about the situation in Spain, and Brecht's drama appeared in different countries. The piece was first played in Paris by Dudow's semi-amateur group of refugee actors in October 1937, and stagings soon followed in Copenhagen, Stockholm, and Prague.[3] In the United States, the People's

Theatre acted the play during April 1938.[4] By September, London's Unity Theatre, which aimed to produce plays for and about workers, delivered the play in a two-hundred seat venue at St Pancras.[5] This latter performance was the very first time that a play by Brecht appeared onstage in Britain.[6]

As a number of critics have noted, this play, which is known in English as *Señora Carrar's Rifles*, broadly provides a retelling of Synge's *Riders to the Sea*, and the story revolves around the central figure of a mother. If Synge had shown the maternal character attempting to stop her son from sailing to sea, Brecht wrote a piece that depicts a similar figure who tries to prevent her two sons from fighting against Franco. It remains unclear how exactly Brecht discovered *Riders to the Sea*, but Susan Cannon Harris suggests that he might have read Werner Wolff's 1935 German translation, or that he may have known Federico García Lorca's 1933 drama *Blood Wedding*, which itself offers a distinctively Spanish variant on Synge's play.[7]

For sure, Brecht knew little about Ireland and Irish culture. But *Señora Carrar's Rifles* nonetheless follows the broad narrative arc of Synge's *Riders to the Sea*. At the end of both plays, the main character witnesses the arrival of her son's corpse, and it is at this point that the two scripts echo one another most closely. In *Riders to the Sea*, Bartley's body is borne by neighbours: '*men carry in the body of BARTLEY, laid on a plank, with a bit of a sail over it, and lay it on the table*'.[8] In *Señora Carrar's Rifles*, Brecht presents an updated version of Synge's scene, revealing how the mother's son Juan has been peacefully fishing, but has been shot by a fascist patrol boat. Juan's body is then carried into the family home: '*Through the open door two fishermen carry the dead body of Juan Carrar on a blood-soaked sailcloth* [...] *The fishermen set the body on the floor*'.[9] At this moment in both plays, then, audiences will find the son's body wrapped in a sail, the presence of the sea, the grieving mother, kneeling, and audible mourning. In the cultural hinterland, of course, lurk the conventions of ancient Greek tragedy, including the offstage deaths of characters, the lamentations of the chorus, and the display of bodies upon the *ekkyklēma*.

But critics have differed in describing the exact nature of the connection between Synge's play and Brecht's. In a single book, the influential critic Martin Esslin asserts both that Brecht's work is '*based* on Synge's *Riders to the Sea*' and that Brecht's drama is '*vaguely* based on Synge's *Riders to the Sea*' [my emphasis].[10] Since then, Anthony Roche has suggested that Brecht created a 'deliberately antithetical' version of Synge's play.[11] Keith Dickson has stated that Brecht envisaged Synge's script as a 'counter-project' to both *Señora Carrar's Rifles* and *Mother Courage*'.[12] Meanwhile Cannon Harris has argued that Brecht produced a version of Synge's script because of the limitations Brecht had faced after fleeing Nazi Germany in 1933, after which he dealt with amateur groups whose members potentially lacked the political and artistic capacity to handle a fully developed kind of epic theatre (a form of theatre evolved by Brecht that avoids mimetic illusion and presents a series of non-linear scenes that seek to raise the social and political understanding of the audience).[13] Such debate about the connection between Synge and Brecht may derive, at least in part, from the fact that Synge's tragedy is quite different from the sort of theatre that Brecht had been advocating. Indeed, Brecht repeatedly expressed downright antipathy to tragedy. The questions posed by this chapter, therefore, are: what kind of tragic ideas did Brecht deploy in his theatre making, and how did he deploy them?

By contrast with Synge, Brecht's thinking about tragedy owes a considerable debt to the ideas of Marx and Hegel. In 1857–8, Karl Marx drafted the *Grundrisse der Kritik der Politischen Ökonomie* ('Fundamentals of Political Economy'), an abandoned critique of political economy that formed the preparatory work for *Das Kapital*. In the *Grundrisse*, Marx wrote of the way in which sophisticated Greek art managed to emerge in an ancient society that remained relatively undeveloped:

Let us take e.g. the relation of Greek art and then of Shakespeare to the present time. It is well known that Greek mythology is not only the arsenal of Greek art but also its foundation. Is the view of nature and of social relations on which the Greek imagination and hence Greek [mythology] is based possible with self-acting mule spindles and railways and locomotives and electrical telegraphs? What chance has Vulcan against Roberts & Co., Jupiter against the lightning-rod and Hermes against the Crédit Mobilier? All mythology overcomes and dominates and shapes the forces of nature in the imagination and by the imagination; it therefore vanishes with the advent of real mastery over them. What becomes of Fama alongside Printing House Square [where *The Times* was printed in London]? Greek art presupposes Greek mythology, i.e. nature and the social forms already reworked in an unconsciously artistic way by the popular imagination.[14]

Marx never moved on to the promised discussion of Shakespeare, but he did use his knowledge of Hegel to elaborate some points about Greek art. Hegel had outlined the idea that the modern world made things different from that of the ancient Greeks because physical phenomena could now be explained by 'universal laws and forces', and because modern understanding was affected by reason, whereas 'the Greek poets looked for the Divine everywhere'.[15] Although Marx also felt that something profound had changed between the realm of the ancient Greeks and the modern day, he believed that what really differentiated his world from theirs was primarily a set of technological developments, which meant the natural world could now be harnessed and controlled by man. Marx saw that a simple ancient society had allowed consciousness to predominate and so had developed a powerful art, but that, in the modern world, imagination had been superseded by the clout of man's technological control over nature. People cannot really appreciate the god of the forge in an era when a commercial organization like Roberts & Co manufactures hundreds of machines to facilitate industrial production on a massive scale.

Brecht discovered this part of Marx's writing in a book published by political philosopher Karl Korsch during 1922, and crucially, in around 1932, Brecht responded with the piece 'Key Points in Korsch, pp.37 and 54'.[16] Brecht's thinking here underpins much of his critique of tragedy, which he elaborated in various writings throughout his life.[17] Brecht agreed that the technological ability of the modern world had overcome natural forces, and thus transcended old mythologies. Yet Brecht also saw that, in contemporary art, certain playwrights were nonetheless borrowing from old Greek ideas, especially the notion of 'pity' from Aristotle. There was a problem here, because such Aristotelian ideas depend on accepting the pre-modern notion that the realm of nature is something which humanity cannot change and cannot master. As Brecht put it:

> In order to gain intellectual credibility for their experiments – itself no easy task – the Naturalists excavated pity from the Aristotelian formula for tragedy. But Aristotelian pity is triggered by absolute conformity with natural laws. It is the aspect, turned towards humanity, of consent with those things humanity cannot change.[18]

Aristotelian notions of tragedy led to a kind of fatalism, with people believing that things were given, and subscribing to a set of 'natural laws' which provided a shared reality and understanding. Resisting tragedy, then, might become radical and subversive. As Brecht put it, 'In our day, struggling against tragedy, just like struggling against religion, is a revolutionary task'.[19]

If that was Brecht's view of tragedy, then his decision to rely on J.M. Synge's work to form the spine of *Senora Carrar's Rifles* looks counterintuitive. After all, Synge's *Riders to the Sea* gives an Aristotelian catharsis and refuses to show that the life of Aran is something that can be changed. The islanders do not look at their situation and suggest any alteration of material, social or political conditions. The characters of Synge's drama

simply face a 'natural' or inexorable fate. Indeed, they remain
entirely helpless in the face of that fate, and Maurya's final
words in the play are those of resignation and acceptance, 'No
man at all can be living for ever, and we must be satisfied'.[20]
Brecht, by contrast, advocated a drama in which the spectator
would feel the opposite, where audiences would, in his famous
formulation of 1935, realize that 'That's not the way [...] It's
got to stop – The sufferings of this man appal me, because
they are unnecessary'.[21] Synge could have written a version of
Riders to the Sea that explicitly emphasized the indifference
of those colonial decision-makers who allowed the continuing
impoverishment of remote communities in rural Ireland, and
he could have created a play that agitated openly for Ireland's
political independence from the Westminster government. But
that is not the play that Synge chose to write. Instead, Synge
wrote a script, obeying the classical unities, in which the
characters cannot avoid what is to come. The plot conclusion
of *Riders to the Sea* is, ultimately, the expected order of things,
with Bartley's inevitable death being foreshadowed throughout
the piece.

Brecht could scarcely have endorsed such a script. For one
thing, he rejected mimetic illusionism on the stage. For another,
in his theoretical writings about tragedy he expressed hatred
towards the idea that destiny was unalterable, and wanted
to show that, by taking action in the present, people could
avoid any tragic sense of inevitability. Brecht wrote some of
his strongest words about this topic after the horrors of the
Second World War. In the ancient world, Aristotle had written
six treatises on logic that his followers grouped together as
his 'Organon' (meaning 'instrument' or 'tool'). Now, in 1948,
Brecht wrote his 'Short Organon for the Theatre' which
condemns theatrical tragedy because it:

> shows the structure of society (represented on the stage) as
> incapable of being influenced by society (in the auditorium).
> Oedipus, who has sinned against certain principles
> underpinning the society of his time, is executed, the gods

see to that, they are beyond criticism. Shakespeare's great individuals, bearing in their breast the stars of their fate, carry out inexorably their futile and deadly rampages, they destroy themselves, life, not death, becomes obscene as they reach breaking point, the catastrophe is beyond criticism. Human sacrifices, all around! Barbaric delights! We know that the barbarians have their kind of art. Let's produce a different one![22]

Brecht deployed over-the-top rhetoric here (including some doubtful moments: Oedipus is scarcely 'executed'), but the playwright did so because he felt tragedy formed part of an entertainment industry that strove to dull audiences and dissuade them from altering unjust circumstances. Theatre thus risked existing as part of the 'bourgeois narcotics industry'. If the sufferings of the tragic protagonist are inevitable, then such a form scarcely provides the opportunity for what Brecht believed central to drama: the exploration of how social change might be enacted. The unfortunate thing about tragedy, as Brecht explained in 'Key Points in Korsch', was that it aligned with social conservatism (why struggle to change things if an inevitable fate governs your life anyway?), and also tended to exclude the working class from the realm of high art. King Lear suffers a fall into beggary, and that is tragic, in part at least, because of his initially exalted status. But there is something quite different in the doom of people who have nothing to lose, and who have never had, and never will have, any hope of attaining a higher position in society. As Brecht put it: 'The tragic does not only characterise a stabilised society, but also presupposes the concepts of high and low'.[23]

Indeed, where members of the proletariat *were* involved as protagonists in modern drama, Brecht argued that what was being presented scarcely qualified as tragedy. In 'Key Points in Korsch', Brecht mentioned Gerhart Hauptmann's 1892 play, *The Weavers*, in which powerless Silesian weavers launch an uprising with no hope of success, and which features a final scene where a stray bullet accidentally hits and kills an old man who is unaffiliated with the uprising. As Ronald Gray puts it, this 'could well have aroused in Brecht the feeling that such fatalistic acquiescence was typical of the whole theatre which he needed to combat'.[24] If Marx had argued that belief in the awe-inspiring power of Jupiter had been superseded by a technological age of lightning conductors, so Brecht observed that the sad fate of impoverished characters in naturalistic drama 'can no longer be found tragic, and thus cannot be passed off as tragic either, in an age which can account for these catastrophes in terms of a mere lack of civilisation, for whose remedy it has already worked out eminently practical suggestions'.[25] Brecht felt that tragedy, with all of its ideas of unchangeable fate and destiny, could not really exist in a scientific age in which technology allows humankind to alter and mitigate an array of once-fixed circumstances.

For example, although Brecht did not comment on this directly, the characters of Synge's *Riders to the Sea* repeatedly drown, and the scientific solution is to replace their precarious coracles with motorized boats for travel to the mainland; to erect warning-signs along the most dangerous parts of the coastline; to shift the local economy away from agricultural production and towards a focus on tourism; and to connect the islands with more advanced forms of communication and weather forecasting (all of which happened, in real life, on the Aran islands during the twentieth century). In these circumstances, to persist in seeing the disasters of *Riders to the Sea* as somehow inescapable was obtuse. Rather than saying 'we must be satisfied', Mauyra should have been saying 'going forward, how can we proactively deploy modern technology to make a step-change in this situation?'. Hegel had encouraged an approach to tragedy that historicized the phenomenon rather than seeing it as transcendent, with Marx and Brecht following this line of thought. As Brecht put it in the early 1940s, at a time when the misfortunes of the war could be blamed on a set of political decisions rather than on anything necessarily inevitable, 'Tragic impact no longer arises (i.e. a noticeable lack of tragic impact becomes apparent) once the great round-up has lost its fatalistic character and come within range of society'.[26]

When Brecht came to adapt *Riders to the Sea*, then, he made key changes in order to avoid the conventions of tragedy that he so disliked. Synge's play does, after all, end on a note of resignation: earlier in Synge's script the mother may have had a choice about whether or not to bless her child, but by the end she can do little but mourn and bear witness. Death has seized her only surviving son, but rather than reflecting upon those precise circumstances, Maurya simply observes that, in the end, death comes for everyone.

Brecht did something quite different in his adaptation of the play. At the end of Brecht's *Señora Carrar's Rifles*, the mother figure learns of her son's demise. But once that body is brought to her, the mother in Brecht's play analyses the contextual reasons why he has died, and then converts to militancy to prevent such a situation repeating in the future. She ejects those around her who wish to pray, and encourages the young to fight, even opting to battle against fascism herself:

The Mother (*simply*)   Blame it on his cap.

First Fisherman   What do you mean?

The Mother   It's shabby. Not like a gentleman's.

First Fisherman   But they can't just loose off at everybody with a shabby cap.

The Mother   Yes they can. They're not human. They're a canker and they've got to be burned out like a canker.

(*To the praying women, politely*)

I'd like you to leave now. I have a few things to do and, as you see, my brother is with me.

The people leave.

[...]

The Mother (*going to the oven in front, loudly*)   Take the
guns! Get ready, José! The bread's done too.

*While The Worker takes the rifles from the box she looks
after the bread. She takes it out of the oven, wraps it in a
cloth and goes over to the men. She reaches for one of the
rifles.*[27]

In Britain, critics did not quite know what to make of this
drama, which had largely, until these closing moments, been
encouraging its audience to share the feelings of the fictional
characters much as Synge's tragedy does. But the end of Brecht's
play shifted to something different, encouraging the audience
members not to empathize with the main character but to
engage intellectually with the broader situation, to think about
class warfare and its signifiers, and to consider how to respond
in practical terms to the contemporary political situation. After
all, at around the time he wrote *Señora Carrar's Rifles* Brecht
had been working on *Lehrstücke* ('learning plays'), which aim
to abolish the division between performance and audience,
to educate individuals into becoming part of a collective,
and to find ways of learning that are adequate for a society in
transition from capitalism to socialism. As Brecht put it, the
Lehrstücke would set forth 'actions so as to call for a critical
approach, so that they would not be taken for granted by the
spectator and would arouse him to think'.[28]

However, the style of *Señora Carrar's Rifles* displeased
critics. 'Men with causes to plead for and injustices to expose
seldom have any hesitation in turning a stage into a platform
and a character into a preacher', complained the *Era*: 'Brecht's
short piece is a passionate outburst on the situation in Spain.
It is sincere and poignant – but not, I am afraid, a play'.[29]
The *New Statesman* expressed similar reservations, declaring,

'*Señora Carrar's Rifles* is very stagey stuff; and the final conversion of the Señora has all the improbable pathos of a leopard changing its spots'.[30]

Brecht himself considered that perhaps, in following *Riders to the Sea*, he had incorporated too many ideas from Aristotelian tragedy, and felt that the deficiencies of this technique would need mitigating in performances of *Señora Carrar's Rifles*. He wrote, likely drawing on Erwin Piscator, 'The drawbacks of this technique can be compensated, up to a point, by presenting the play together with a documentary film on the events in Spain, or by linking it with some propagandistic occasion'.[31] Accordingly, when Brecht's play appeared onstage across the UK in 1938 and 1939, it was given a deliberately politicized context. In Northumberland, for example, it appeared at a Miners' Hall under the auspices of the Prudhoe Left Book Club and the Newcastle Left Theatre Guild.[32] At Falkirk, the Unity Theatre presented the piece alongside a dramatized poem, 'Spain Fights Back', during which the members of the company gave the Communist salute and sang the 'Internationale'.[33] In Edinburgh, Brecht's play moved towards agit-prop when it appeared at the Central Halls, where an appeal was made on behalf of starving children in Spain. This Scottish audience heard that 'thousands of children on the Government side would die this winter' and a collection was made for the assistance of civilian refugees. A local clergyman, who presided at the Edinburgh performance, also gave a prescient address, in which he declared that 'the issue involved in the Spanish War was whether we could afford to let policies grow which grew on the destruction of free peoples and the strengthening of tyrants'.[34]

Brecht feared that such political lessons could be lost in a theatre dominated by the old, Aristotelian notion of catharsis, which, as he famously put it, encouraged the spectator to think, 'That's great art [...] I weep when they weep; I laugh when they laugh'.[35] To Brecht's mind, such a response prevented audiences from seeing the play's action from anything other than the perspective of the main character, and so blocked spectators from comprehending a work's broader social significance. An audience whose members shared the emotions apparently being experienced by a fictional stage character would potentially focus excessively on upset and suffering. In that scenario, the audience would have a reduced capacity for questioning why that suffering was happening in the first place, and would remain unlikely to take action to end such situations in real life. Brecht realized that the affective reach of tragedy had the potential to diminish the epic effect for which he strove, and he noted approvingly that, when Helene Weigel played Jocasta's servant in *Oedipus Rex* during 1929, the actor had announced the death of Jocasta 'in a completely emotionless, piercing voice' that sought to involve the audience 'in the intellectual decisions that make up the action' rather than involving spectators in 'an opportunity for new emotions'.[36] By contrast, after Weigel (who had since married Brecht) played the mother in *Señora Carrar's Rifles* in Dudow's Paris production in 1937, Brecht observed: 'Even Weigel herself on some occasions broke into tears at certain passages [...] tears came into her eyes as she delivered her condemnation of her son, who was already murdered'. But Brecht satisfied himself that Weigel 'wept not as a peasant woman, but as a performer over the peasant woman'.[37] He also took pains to record a conversation he had with another actor (possibly Per Knutzon) about Weigel's latter performance:

Me [...] She didn't create any illusion that she *was* the fisherman's wife.

The Actor [...] I'm sure she had developed a complete technique for sustaining this feeling in the audience, the feeling that she is not what she portrays.

Me Do you think you could describe such a technique?

The Actor Suppose she had tacitly thought 'And then the fisherman's wife said' before every sentence, then that

sentence would have emerged very much as it did. What
I mean is, she was plainly speaking another woman's words.

Me Perfectly right. And why do you make her say 'said'?
Why put it in the past tense?

The Actor Because it's equally plain that she was re-
enacting something that had happened in the past; in other
words, the spectator is under no illusion that it's happening
now or that he himself is witnessing the original incident.[38]

For the Swedish production of the play, which took place
after the fall of the Spanish Republic in March 1939, Brecht
attempted to move his tragedy further away from Aristotle,
adding a prologue which takes place in a French internment
camp for Spanish refugees. Here Señora Carrar and her
brother are held behind barbed wire, allowing Brecht to situate
the Spanish conflict within a wider European context (the new
opening line of the play is 'It's all come out now about why
the Czechoslovakian Republic didn't fight when the Germans
invaded').[39] This prologue also meant that the main drama was
put into flashback, at a point before Señora Carrar arrived in
the internment camp, and thus allowed Brecht to make clear
that the events are occurring in the past: the spectator should
be 'under no illusion that it's happening now or that he himself
is witnessing the original incident'.[40] Brecht also added an
epilogue to the piece, which featured Señora Carrar's brother
('the Worker') contextualizing the action that the audience had
just seen, and promising that rifles will be brought out again
to fight injustice.[41]

Aristotle's *Poetics* may have indicated that tragedy involved
the realization of universal truths about human existence. But
Brecht did not wish to suggest that the mother's experience is
common to everyone (as Synge's play does to an extent, pointing
out that everyone is mortal and so '*we* must be satisfied' [my
emphasis]). Brecht's version of the story encourages spectators
to think about how the mother's sense of grief is generated in

a very particular set of cultural and historical circumstances, and about how people should be ready to fight against similar inequities in the future.

If Brecht had to make such changes to the ending of Synge's play, why, then, did Brecht bother with the idea of tragedy at all? Why not create his own theatre from an entirely different form? During the initial stages of the Second World War, Brecht began work on a diffuse corpus of theoretical writings about the theatre, which would eventually be published in German in 1963, in the fifth volume of Brecht's *Writings on Theatre* edited by Werner Hecht, and in English in 1965, translated by John Willett as *The Messingkauf Dialogues*, which translates literally as *Buying Brass*. There remain scholarly disagreements about what should really be included in *Buying Brass*, but nonetheless, part of this theoretical thinking that Brecht worked on between early 1939 and early 1941 includes a discussion of theatrical tragedy, in which he discusses how tragedy could be reinvented to suit the modern era. The philosopher in Brecht's dialogue states that the old Aristotelian ideas of pity and terror might still prove salient for modern dramatists and audiences, but only if the terms were redefined to take on a less individualistic and more communal implication. In the *Poetics*, Aristotle had asserted that, in tragic drama, the feelings of pity and fear might serve to purge the emotions of the audience and have a cathartic effect. Brecht's philosopher asserts:

> For the ancients, the object of tragedy was to inspire pity and terror. That could still be a desirable object nowadays, if pity were taken to mean pity for people, and terror to mean terror of people, and if serious theatre were thus to help eliminate those conditions in which people need to pity and fear one another.[42]

In an era of modern technology, when remote warfare allows for the destruction of entire nations, the philosopher argues that drama needs to be updated, to make clear that the theatre is not only about individuals but about groups:

The opponents can confront each other on the stage. A lot of technical changes will be needed, of course. Many human characteristics and passions that used to be important have become irrelevant. On the other hand, others have taken their place. In any case, it's difficult to grasp very much without seeing beyond individuals to the major group conflicts.[43]

In another 1939–41 section of *Buying Brass*, Brecht addresses the topic of Shakespearean tragedy, again emphasizing that these plays should not simply be seen as describing the fall of a great man or the fate of an individual, but that those works concern profound shifts in society:

Dramaturg   What about tragedy in Shakespeare?'

Philosopher   Shakespeare takes a tragic view of the decline of feudalism […]

Actor   To many people that explanation might make the plays seem rather trite.

Philosopher   But how could there be anything more multifaceted, fascinating and important than the decline of great ruling classes?[44]

Thus, Brecht found that a reinvented kind of tragedy might prove relevant in the twentieth century, if only the idea of tragedy might be recontextualized and rethought.

This idea about recontextualizing tragedy is important, because although Brecht wrote in often scathing terms about the tragic, he repeatedly utilized existing ideas and concepts of tragedy in his own plays. *Señora Carrar's Rifles* was no one-off. In 1928, Brecht praised Georg Büchner's *Woyzeck* (published posthumously in 1879), the play in which a German soldier suffers a mental breakdown and kills his wife (and which was described by Steiner as 'the first real tragedy of low life') as 'technically almost perfect', and Brecht's work repeatedly follows something of *Woyzeck*'s episodic structure.[45] As G.E. Nelson points out, Brecht's *Mother Courage*, *Saint Joan of the Stockyards*, and *Life of Galileo* can be viewed as successful modern tragedies.[46] Brecht repeatedly criticized what he saw as the inappropriate application of ancient Greek cultural ideas, which could scarcely work in a modern technological age, but also relied upon those ideas in order to develop his own sense of theatre. Simon Goldhill remarks:

> I think one could make a case for Brecht having learned a good deal from Sophocles, and in particular from the device of dramatizing an audience on stage. The effect of putting an audience on stage is to provide a mirror to the audience of its own processes of reaction. It works to distance the audience from a direct emotional absorption and see itself watching.[47]

Goldhill here emphasizes that, quite aside from any philosophical ideas about tragedy, Brecht was happy to pilfer theatrical conventions from Greek tragedy as part of a rejection of mimetic illusionistic theatre. Indeed, Brecht himself admitted that 'Greek dramaturgy uses certain forms of *Verfremdung*, notably interventions by the chorus'.[48] The staging of Shakespearean tragedy on the Elizabethan and Jacobean stage had a similarly significant effect upon the practical stagecraft that Brecht employed. In general terms, the direct address repeatedly employed by Brecht's characters and his use of a bare stage recall the performance style of the King's Men. More directly, the language of *Saint Joan of the Stockyards* offers a clever Shakespearean pastiche, in 1927 and 1941 Brecht adapted *Macbeth* and *Hamlet* for radio, whilst in 1948 he proposed a *King Lear* project.[49]

By the end of 1947, Brecht had even begun to work on his own classical tragedy, a version of Sophocles' *Antigone* which would first appear onstage the following year at Chur in Switzerland. But, as with his earlier adaptation of Synge,

Brecht's use of Sophocles sought to reinvent aspects of the existing tragic form. Brecht's version of *Antigone* adds a prelude which takes place at the end of the Second World War, in Berlin during the final days of Hitler's regime. Here we find two sisters who return to their home from an air-raid shelter. They repeatedly hear screaming outside, and one of the sisters then discovers their brother strung from a meat hook.[50] Their brother has deserted from the German army, and as a result has been hanged, with one of the sisters vowing to cut down his body. An SS man appears, and asks the two sisters if they know the identity of the treacherous dead man. Although the first sister issues a Petrine denial, the officer asks why the second sister is holding a knife. The prelude ends with the first sister declaring:

> Then I looked at my sister.
> Should she on pain of death go now
> And free our brother who
> May be dead or no?[51]

The audience observes as the characters face their dilemma: will the sisters dare to cut down their brother, as the SS officer looks on, or not?

At that point, the prelude ends and the familiar story of *Antigone* begins. The prelude obviously echoes the narrative told by Sophocles, in which Antigone and her sister wish to bury their brother, whose body has been left shamefully uninterred on the battlefield by command of Creon, the ruler of Thebes. But as Brecht had done with his earlier adaptation of Synge's work, the German playwright again brought earlier tragedy into contact with specific, contemporary events. When the prelude of Brecht's *Antigone* moves into the main play, the scene shifts from Berlin in April 1945 to outside Creon's palace in ancient Thebes. Brecht's friend, Walter Benjamin, wrote, 'The epic theater has a relation to the passing of time which is entirely different from that of the tragic theater. Because its suspense is a function less of the dénouement than of particular scenes, the epic theater can cover enormous spans of time'.[52] If Synge's *Riders to the Sea* tells the story of just a few hours and entirely stays within one family's homestead, Brecht's *Antigone* ranges over more than two thousand kilometres and spans two and a half thousand years.

Most notably, in his updated version of *Antigone*, Brecht changed the storyline of the original drama by Sophocles (and of the earlier German translation by Hölderlin, upon which Brecht relied). In Brecht's version, Creon is the ruler of the city of Thebes who has embarked upon an offensive war to gain the manufacturing resources of a metal-rich neighbour, Argos. In Brecht's adaptation, Creon is repeatedly addressed, early in the play, as 'mein Führer'/'Führer'.[53] Brecht's play also makes repeated reference to the national socialist term 'Stürme' to describe the troops of Thebes. We find, for instance, the bloody description: '*Die Stürme, von dem Blutbad in den eignen/ Reihn noch nicht ausgeschlafen, hoben müd nur/ Die Beile, nass noch von thebanischem Blut/ Wider das Argosvolk*' ('Our stormtroops, not having slept enough after/ The bloodbath in their own ranks, raised only wearily/ Their axes wet still with the blood of Thebans/ Against the people of Argos').[54] But by the end of the play, this Führer's ambitions have led to Theban destruction. In this way, Brecht encourages audiences to compare Thebes's annihilation under Creon with the concluding devastation of Hitler's rule.

In Sophocles' play, Creon might win our sympathies. As Hegel emphasizes, the drama is finely balanced between Creon's obligation to run an orderly city, and Antigone's duty towards her family and her religion. With Sophocles' version of the tale, it is possible for an audience to experience benign feelings towards Creon, whose aim in maintaining civic stability is laudable. But Brecht's retelling makes it wellnigh impossible to sympathize with the Creon-as-Hitler figure. Here, Creon, the autocrat, has pursued war in order to obtain iron which he can use for weaponry. In Sophocles' play, Creon is guilty of ignoring the gods and their notions of justice, but in Brecht's version of *Antigone*, the gods are removed from their central position and Creon's crime revolves around how he behaves towards people: 'Humanity/ Weighs with him not a jot. Monstrous thereby/ He becomes to himself'.[55] Antigone, too, in Brecht's version of the play, says something quite different from her counterpart in Sophocles' work. In the original text she praises divine laws as being superior to human laws, but in Brecht's drama she has little time for prescriptions from the gods, declaring, 'I'd rather have it/ Human and humane'.[56]

For Sophocles, Antigone was born into the doomed house of Labdacus, she was the daughter of Oedipus, and so she suffers an inevitable fate. But Brecht challenges that sense of inevitability, drawing attention to the wider circumstances of imperialist war and asking whether the characters could have acted differently in order to change the outcome of the drama. Indeed, he asks questions about the culpability of the wider city. The chorus of Elders has supported Creon because of self-interest when they could potentially have resisted ('We heard/ Many a bad thing [...] and stopped our ears').[57] Antigone herself acts, but acts late. As Brecht's chorus points out, she was complicit with Creon until her brother's death, and so audiences may have noted parallels with real-life figures such as the once-Hitler supporting Claus Schenk Graf von Stauffenberg, a nobleman who tried to assassinate the Führer in 1944. More generally, Brecht's version of *Antigone* implies that, if a greater number of soldiers had deserted, the final ruin of Thebes could have been averted, again pointing to similarities with the fall of Germany under Hitler. Tom Kuhn and David Constantine emphasize that:

> Brecht can and does 'rationalise' the story of *Antigone*, removing from it all notions of fate and predestination. But in the end the chief topicality of the subject for him is Creon's crazed violence: the degree of violence necessary to fight an unjust war and control the home population whilst doing so. Creon, like Hitler, learning nothing, drags down the state – which in his view has failed him – in his own catastrophe.[58]

Brecht's version of *Antigone* premiered in Chur during 1948. At this moment, then, Brecht had shown how the tragic impulse could be rooted in a specific place and time, could speak of individual calamity in the context of the collective, and could have an intellectual rather than an empathetic effect, with Brecht utilizing tragic ideas for raising political awareness and combating injustice.

However, by this point in the twentieth century, another playwright who would have great influence had shown himself willing to operate in a different philosophical tradition than that of Brecht. In his 1930 essay *Proust*, Samuel Beckett had written:

> Tragedy is not concerned with human justice. Tragedy is the statement of an expiation, but not the expiation of a codified breach of local arrangement, organised by the knaves for the fools. The tragic figure represents the expiation of original sin, of the original and eternal sin of him and all his 'socii malorum', the sin of having been born.[59]

If Brecht's drama situated tragedy in a realm of the particulars, with its stormtroopers and its Führer, Beckett argued that tragedy has little to do with any 'breach of local arrangement' but was instead about the far more widely shared problem of the human condition itself, 'the sin of having been born'.

Here Beckett drew on the thought of Schopenhauer, the nineteenth-century philosopher whose deeply pessimistic *Weltanschauung* contrasts with the more optimistic thinking of Hegel. Schopenhauer wrote about tragedy in *The World as Will and Representation* (1818), where he wondered why people can possibly find pleasure in watching fictional depictions of events that would be highly disagreeable in real life. Schopenhauer saw that theatrical tragedy was 'the pinnacle of literature', yet, in such literature, audiences are presented with the most appalling suffering.[60] How could that experience possibly be relished?

Schopenhauer offered the answer that tragedy reflected the 'essence of the world', an essence which was cruel and punishing even to those who had apparently done no wrong, and that any 'demand for so-called poetic justice' in drama simply reflected an audience's desire to block its ears to the world's true nature.[61] He commented:

> The true sense of tragedy is the deeper insight that the hero does not atone for his particular sins, but for original sin instead, i.e. the guilt of existence itself:
>> Because the greatest offence of man,
>> Is that he was born
> as Calderón says with perfect frankness.[62]

During his early twenties, Beckett proved himself an enthusiastic reader of Schopenhauer, recognizing an affinity with the German's glum philosophizing. In particular, Beckett felt moved by that idea of 'the sin of having been born', which Schopenhauer was recycling from the seventeenth-century Spanish poet and playwright Pedro Calderón de la Barca. Beckett, having discovered these words in Schopenhauer, would later reuse them when writing about Proust.[63] Beckett may also have realized that Calderón's sentiment resonates with the thinking of the chorus in *Oedipus at Colonus*. After all, when Beckett had been a student at Trinity College Dublin, he had watched Yeats's versions of *King Oedipus* and *Oedipus at Colonus*, with the Yeatsian adaptation of the latter piece including the choral line, 'Never to have lived is best'.[64]

Such ideas would long remain with Beckett, and after he included them in his essay about Proust they would subsequently echo in his best-known dramatic work. Hence, in *Waiting for Godot*, we find the following exchange:

Vladimir   Suppose we repented.

Estragon   Repented what?

Vladmir   Oh [...] We wouldn't have to go into the details.

Estragon   Our being born?[65]

Other moments in Beckett's work also carry a hint of Greek tragedy. For example, George Steiner finds a connection between *Godot* and the *Oresteia*, whilst Barry Allen Spence connects *Happy Days* with the *Agamemnon*, and observes that Beckett's 'theatrical work resonates with the notion of Greek tragedy as the medium that unflinchingly presents the spectacle of human misery'.[66]

But Beckett's reading of classical tragedy followed a different route from that of Brecht. In the Beckett archive we can find the unpublished notes that the Irish dramatist made during the 1930s about tragic Greek playwriting. Although Beckett lists the titles of the extant works by the ancient dramatists, he does not discuss the plots of those works at all, and says very little about their form (simply noting that Aeschylus is the 'first to introduce 2 actors besides choruses').[67] Instead, Beckett's notes focus on the biographies of the three most famous Attic tragedians, and devotes most of his attention to their personal misfortunes and deaths. Hence, Beckett describes Aeschylus in the following way:

> Face ferocious when composing.
> Accused of drinking to excess, never wrote except when drunk.
> In old age retired to court of Hiero in Sicily. Being informed that he was to die by the fall of a house, he retired from city into fields, where he sat down. An eagle, ~~supposing~~ taking his bald head for a stone, dropped upon it a tortoise, & he died of the blow.[68]

When Beckett came to describe Sophocles, he noted the 'Famous ingratitude of his children who accused him of insanity. In defence of which he read his <u>Oedipus at Colonus</u>'.[69] Similarly, when Beckett wrote of Euripides he wrote, 'MISOGYNIST.

Twice married & divorced', and also noted: 'Rivalry with Sophocles. Fled from Athens to court of Archelaus King of Macedonia. Torn to pieces by dogs of Archelaus during one of his solitary walks'.[70] Brecht had felt inspired by what he had learned of Sophocles in order to say something about the structure of war and politics in the modern era, but Beckett, in those notes on tragedy, instead focused on something far smaller in scale, the individual miseries and bleak ironies of the tragedians' own lives. In Aeschylus, Beckett saw a man who may have depicted the fall of the house of Atreus, but whose own death arrived with a falling tortoise's house. Sophocles may have depicted the familial loyalty of Antigone, but his own children thought him mad; and Euripides' desire for solitude brought him only into contact with a crowd of marauding and murderous hounds.

Beckett saw the Greek tragedians through the prism of relatively workaday sorrows, including the alcoholism of Aeschylus, the ungrateful offspring of Sophocles, and the marital disappointments of Euripides. These notes about ancient Greek tragedy dovetail with Beckett's broader philosophical attitude towards tragedy. When Beckett studied Schopenhauer he encountered a philosopher who described how there were broadly three categories which portrayed the misfortune necessary for tragedy. In the first category, an extraordinary evil was to blame for catastrophe, such as the malevolence of Richard III, or Iago in *Othello*. In the second category, blind fate was responsible for misfortune, as in *Romeo and Juliet* or *The Women of Trachis*. But in the third category, Schopenhauer described how:

Finally, misfortune can also be introduced simply by means of people's positioning with respect to each other, through their relationships; so that there is no need for a terrible mistake or unheard-of accident or even for a character whose evilness extends to the limits of human possibility; instead, morally ordinary characters in everyday circumstances are positioned with respect to each other in such a way that their situation forces them knowingly and clear-sightedly to cause each other the greatest harm without the injustice falling on one side or the other.[71]

Schopenhauer felt this last type of tragedy was preferable because the other kinds of tragedy only threaten us from a distance. How often, after all, are we likely to encounter a Richard III? How often are we likely to fall in love with the scion of our family's sworn enemy? By contrast, the final type of tragedy shows the kind of powers and entanglements that could affect almost any person at any time. Watching this version of the tragic in a playhouse means that 'we shudder as we feel ourselves already in the middle of hell'. However, such tragedy, although potentially the most effective, also creates considerable difficulties for the dramatist, 'because it has to produce the greatest effect merely by positioning and distribution, with the least expenditure of means and the smallest number of causes of action'.[72]

In 1953, Beckett premiered *Waiting for Godot*, which focused very little on any causes of action. Previously, 'drama' had been largely synonymous with action, as Hegel explained in his *Lectures on Aesthetics*: 'What after all is effective in drama is the action as action and not the exposure of the character as such independently of his specific aim and achievement'.[73] But Beckett comes closer to what Maeterlinck called *drame statique*. In *Waiting for Godot*, we find two figures who do not seem to know very basic details about their lives, who cannot recall what they have done in the past, and who do not know what action to take in the present ('what do we do now?', they repeatedly implore). The two main characters mainly spend their time waiting for someone who fails to arrive, amusing themselves as best they can, and making a final, botched attempt at suicide.

Jon Erickson argues that '*Waiting for Godot* can be seen as a modern tragedy, although what is tragic in modernism is less the linear arrow of Aristotelian downfall than a sense of ongoing and circular futility'.[74] Of course, the obvious question then arises of whether futility is really tragic, and, as noted in the introduction to this book, some critics have wondered whether this play really qualifies as tragedy at all. K.M. Newton, for example, makes the Hegelian suggestion that 'the fundamental difference between Beckett and the tragic as used in critical and philosophical discussion is that there is no conflict or collision between opposed positions in Beckett'.[75] Beckett himself avoided calling the play a tragedy, instead labelling it a 'tragicomedy', which as Axel Kruse suggests, might be 'characteristic of his wit. *Waiting for Godot* is a study of the nature of tragedy, and exercise of wit about the idea that tragedy is dead'.[76]

The plays by Bertolt Brecht that this chapter has examined, and which, in performance, physicalize his theoretical ideas of tragedy, are set in specific places and at recognizable times. When Brecht followed Synge, he created, in *Señora Carrar's Rifles*, a drama set largely during the Spanish Civil War and concluding with a ringing call for political action. In this way, Brecht presented an ultimately utopian scenario in which individuals can strive to understand and then change their circumstances. But Samuel Beckett had also studied Synge closely, and had been led to a very different set of artistic conclusions. Indeed, Beckett's biographer, James Knowlson, noted that performances of 'John Millington Synge's plays at the Abbey were of greater significance to Beckett than the work of any other Irish dramatists. When I asked him who he himself felt had influenced his own theatre most of all, he suggested only the name of Synge'.[77] But despite this shared influence, Beckett's art leaves the audience in a contrasting place from that of Brecht. Brecht sought to use Synge's plot and to include an affirmative ending that suggested the possibility of political change. Yet Beckett realized, as Jon Erickson points out, that:

> politics won't prevent you from dying, even if the right kind of political choices can prevent the premature or 'senseless' death that may come from the wrong political choices. Whatever is performed at the end with regard to the social

factors of gender, colour, or class, and the respect or non-respect paid to them, death itself is no respecter of persons, of whatever gender, colour, or class. It is at this level that Beckett is operating.[78]

When J.M. Synge wrote *Riders to the Sea* he presented an irrevocable fate that unspooled exactly as anticipated by the main character, and there may be an echo of Schopenhauer in this aspect of Synge's thinking. After all, like Beckett, Synge had also read Schopenhauer, spending time on 6 April 1893 examining 'An Essay on Visions and Matters Connected Therewith', in which the German reflected on the 'prophetic misgiving' and 'dark foreboding' that people may feel, for example, 'if a man is on the point of going on board a ship which is to perish'.[79] Indeed, such unworldly anticipation of a seafarer's demise was something that Synge returned to and described in *Riders to the Sea*.

Brecht of course felt differently, and had little time for such notions of prophecy and fate. He followed Marx's idea that technological progress meant that humankind had outgrown the perceptions of the ancient Greeks: that the realm of ancient myths 'vanishes with the advent of real mastery over them'.[80] At the end of *Señora Carrar's Rifles*, then, the main character does not simply accept the catastrophic predicament in which she finds herself. She may be launching into a deathly mission, but she has shown the capacity for change and development.

In Beckett's play, the tragedy arises through the fact that no change is possible. Here, the human condition is what it is. The play opens with the line, 'Nothing to be done'.[81] From the start of *Waiting for Godot*, it is clear that no solution can be found to the ontological problem of being alive. Even the play's culminating attempt at self-slaughter results in nothing more than a slapstick gag, leaving the characters caught in a cycle of frustration, uncertainty, and deterioration.

The most famous stage direction of Samuel Beckett's play *Waiting for Godot* is the one that ends both the first and second acts of the play:

Estragon   Well, shall we go?

Vladimir   Yes, let's go.

They do not move.

CURTAIN[82]

Here, the words being spoken do not fit the action being taken. Indeed, the words directly contradict the action. In this way, Beckett ensures that language itself is devalued and decayed, mirroring the decline found elsewhere in the play (Lucky becomes dumb in the second act, Pozzo becomes blind, the vegetables become blackened …). Just as the waiting in the play shows us the senselessness of life, the language of the play shows us the failure of rational discourse. As Schopenhauer put it, 'we have discovered the tendency and ultimate intention of *tragedy* to be a turning towards resignation, towards a negation of the will to life'.[83]

Beckett's closing stage direction therefore offers the binary opposite of the closing stage direction of Brecht's *Señora Carrar's Rifles*:

The Mother (*going to the oven in front, loudly*)   Take the guns! Get ready, José!

[…] *She reaches for one of the rifles*

José   What, you coming too?

The Mother   Yes, for Juan.

They go to the door.[84]

As we know from Ibsen's *A Doll's House*, a closing theatrical movement towards the door offers possibilities of radical change, of escape, of renewal. The ending of *Señora Carrar's*

Rifles offers a way for tragedy to be uplifting, whereas the final stage direction of *Godot* instead follows Schopenhauer's tragic thinking towards resignation, stasis, and repetition.

In real life, Beckett himself had scarcely been passive in the face of adverse political circumstances. He had worked with the French resistance in occupied Europe during the war, even though his Irish citizenship meant he could have escaped to a neutral country. Yet Beckett's drama has generated suspicion from some on the left because it seems to point towards political inertia and powerlessness. Raymond Williams warns that Beckett might be a 'genius' but that Beckett's drama 'reduced the scale of human possibility and human action'.[85]

The worst fears of Williams may appear to have been realized during the early twenty-first century in the work of Vladislav Surkov, a political operator who took careful note of Beckett. Surkov attended the Moscow Institute of Culture, spending three years there as part of a five-year programme in theatre direction. He subsequently worked in PR and became one of President Vladimir Putin's closest advisers. But Surkov did not forget what he had learned in the theatre world. As the documentary filmmaker Adam Curtis has observed of Surkov:

> He came originally from the avant-garde art world, and those who have studied his career say that what Surkov has done is to import ideas from conceptual art into the very heart of politics. His aim is to undermine peoples' perceptions of the world, so they never know what is really happening. Surkov turned Russian politics into a bewildering, constantly changing piece of theatre. He sponsored all kinds of groups, from neo-Nazi skinheads to liberal human rights groups. He even backed parties that were opposed to President Putin. But the key thing was that Surkov then let it be known that this was what he was doing. Which meant that no-one was sure what was real or fake. As one journalist put it: 'It is a strategy of power that keeps any opposition constantly confused'.[86]

As Curtis observes, Surkov intended to create a 'defeatist response' that has 'become a central part of a new system of political control', but which has relied upon Surkov's prior knowledge of theatre. Surkov published a 2009 novel *Almost Zero* which begins by looking back to the setting and the characters of *Waiting for Godot*:

Are you all comfortable? Can everybody see everything? Can everybody see the vast expanse of space into which walk a pair of clowns, a vulgar duo of charlatans, corrupt comics, masters of their craft – their craft simply teasing and mocking, tormenting and taunting – also, at any moment ready to perform tragedy [...] Two clowns emerge; their names Bim and Bom, Yin and Yang, Adam and Eve, Taira and Minamoto, Vladimir and Estragon [...][87]

Like the characters of Beckett's play, the characters of Surkov's *Almost Zero* (which subsequently appeared in dramatized version at the Moscow Arts Theatre during 2011) are bewildered about the situation in which they are living. Central to the plot is the confusion of fictional audience members about whether they are watching authentic events, or whether they are witnessing a fictional simulation of reality. That mystery is wrapped inside *Almost Zero*'s broader enigma about the author's identity: Surkov published the novel under a pseudonym and at one stage declared, 'The author of this novel is an unoriginal Hamlet-obsessed hack'.[88] In real life, as in the theatre, Surkov's political techniques place the audience in a position analogous to Beckett's two main characters, Vladimir and Estragon: that is, terminally unsure about what is going on, unable to decipher anything about the broader social structure of the situation that is being experienced, and left with a sense of the futility of any action. Nothing said or done will have any effect. We may as well tell one another jokes or play games to pass the time.

Other real-life political figures, often expensively schooled in tragic thinking, have realized that a rhetoric of 'tragedy' can have the same politically nullifying effect. For example, in June 2017, after an appalling fire killed seventy-two people in Grenfell Tower, West London, the city's former mayor, Boris Johnson (BA Classics, University of Oxford), who had been responsible for inflicting major budget reductions upon the local emergency services, published a statement to say, 'I find it unbelievable that Labour [his political opponents] are suggesting that this tragedy was somehow caused by fire service cuts'.[89] Likewise, the US presidential candidate, Mitt Romney (BA English, Brigham Young University), who ran for office in the 2012 election and could not afford to alienate gun owners, responded to a mass shooting in Colorado by declaring, 'Our hearts break with the sadness of this unspeakable tragedy'.[90] Following the Black Lives Matter protests of 2019, one perceptive response came from the journalist Jemele Hill, who noted: 'Using the word *tragedy* to describe Breonna Taylor's killing is an insult [...] This description sounded as if the bullets that killed her in her own apartment had mysteriously fallen from the sky and hadn't actually come from the guns of Louisville police'.[91] As Hill emphasizes, the familiar rhetoric of tragedy used on such occasions allows an evasion of accountability. Mourning and remembrance are the approved response, rather than questioning the underlying structures that might have facilitated such deadly outcomes. In this way, tragic thinking might potentially do damage to the citizen's willingness to take action, and so corrode the participative structures of democratic society.

Yet the work of Vladislav Surkov is not the only place that we might find the logical end-point of Beckett's version of tragedy. A number of important critical thinkers have located in Beckett's work at least the potential to engender a positive political response, with his linguistic formulations resisting the kind of homogenizing thought needed to endorse totalitarianism.[92] Meanwhile, any simple binary between a politically sensitized Brecht and a politically indifferent Beckett is increasingly difficult to maintain when we look at recent scholarship on Beckett in particular, and at the way in which both playwrights dealt with the genocide of European Jews during the Second World War. Brecht wrote anti-Nazi satires, *The Resistible Rise of Arturo Ui* and *Round Heads and Pointy Heads*, but these dramas avoid the Holocaust. As Fredric Jameson writes, the latter play 'omits the Jews and seems to fail to grasp what was historically unique in the Nazi politics directed towards them'.[93] In Beckett's work, his characters often avoid racial and historical specificity, but this world nonetheless looks at times like that of the concentration camp. Ira Nadel points out that:

> Elements of *Godot* are rife with Holocaust allusions, from the nightly beatings of Estragon/Gogo, who learns to accept pain as a constant, to the telling question of Vladimir – 'where are all these corpses from?' and the whippings of Lucky which evoke the capos of the concentration camps, as well as the dialogue about dead voices and their need to speak.[94]

In recent years, critics have increasingly highlighted such aspects of Beckett's writing, arguing that, as Emilie Morin puts it, Beckett's texts 'harbour a real political immediacy'.[95]

Indeed, Brecht himself may have realized the political potential of Beckett's writing. At one stage, Brecht read a copy of the 1953 Elmar Tophoven translation of *Waiting for Godot* (*Warten auf Godot*, published by Suhrkamp, Berlin), and set about creating a version of Beckett's play. Brecht wanted the characters of *Godot* to be rooted in real-life social types. Hence, in his adaptation, Estragon was to be a proletarian worker, Vladimir an intellectual, Pozzo would be a landowner called 'von Pozzo' (the 'von' indicating nobility), and Lucky a police officer.[96] That characterization meant that Brecht needed to make other alterations to the text. If Estragon was a worker, then it perhaps made less sense for that character to talk about his holiday plans in the Middle East or about writing poetry, so Brecht edited the following passage, reversing the speaking roles to make the intellectual

Vladimir into the poet (rather than Estragon being the poet as in Beckett's original):

Estragon: I remember the maps of the Holy Land. Coloured they were. ~~Very pretty.~~ The Dead Sea was pale blue. The very look of it made me thirsty. ~~That's where we'll go, I used to say, that's where we'll go for our honeymoon. We'll swim. We'll be happy.~~"

~~**Vladimir:**   You should have been a poet.~~
Estragon: I'm listening. You're supposed to be a poet.

~~**Estragon:**~~
Vladimir: I was. (Gesture towards his rags.) Isn't that obvious?[97]

Elsewhere in the text, Brecht erased some of Estragon's more philosophical, abstract thoughts, and, rather surprisingly for the boxing-fan that Brecht was, deleted the stage direction that describes Estragon making gestures '*like those of a spectator encouraging a pugilist*'.[98] Perhaps Beckett's humour in that particular direction struck too close to home for Brecht. Brecht, after all, suggested that his very early one-act farce *The Wedding* should be set in a boxing ring, he helped with a production of *Little Mahagonny* that took place in a boxing venue, and he suggested that those organizing theatre events should make the actual lights visible just as 'at a sporting event, a boxing match for instance'.[99]

In any event, mid-way through adapting *Godot*, Brecht gave up on the attempt, although in future years he perhaps continued to dwell on Beckett's play. Käthe Rülicke-Weiler reports that shortly before Brecht's death, as he lay in hospital, he hit upon the idea of creating a version of *Godot* where scenes of stasis from Beckett's play would appear in the foreground whilst, in the background, contrasting scenes of revolution from across the world would play as film clips.[100]

Brecht was nothing if not a theatrical magpie, willing to adapt ideas and techniques from a variety of different sources.

When Brecht created a modelbook to help future theatre makers understand how he had created his version of *Antigone* in 1948, he asserted that 'Theatre is simple-minded if it is not multifaceted'.[101] Thus, he appropriated ideas from classical Greek tragedy at the same time that he excoriated Aristotelian catharsis; he adopted the storyline of *Riders to the Sea* at the same time as he strove to create a less emotive and more politically activist finale to the tragic piece; and, although he may have approached the idea of tragedy from a fundamentally different philosophical position than Samuel Beckett, Brecht nonetheless found in Beckett's theatre work a potential for collaboration.

Ultimately then, from a Brechtian perspective, what is the purpose of tragedy? As Brecht himself acknowledged:

> What the ancients, following Aristotle, demanded of tragedy is nothing higher or lower than entertaining people [...] the catharsis of which Aristotle writes, cleansing by fear and pity or from fear and pity, is an ablution which was performed not only in a pleasurable way, but precisely for the purpose of pleasure.[102]

But Brecht wanted more: he felt that in his preferred form of theatre, the epic theatre, spectators should come to see why problems existed, and what could be done to avoid such problems in the future. Tragic ideas could be useful, and might provide inspiration for the theatre maker, but tragedy could not be replicated wholesale without considerable modification and recontextualizing. Brecht's friend Walter Benjamin wrote, 'Tragedies and operas go on and on being written, apparently with a trusty stage apparatus to hand, whereas in reality they do nothing but supply material for an apparatus which is obsolete'.[103] Brecht himself agreed that much of the existing apparatus of the playhouse was outmoded, but nonetheless did utilize certain kinds of tragic paraphernalia in order to reinvigorate the stage, and in the next chapter we shall see how tragic ideas helped to develop the possibilities of drama in locations far from the geographical areas in which tragedy and tragic thinking first developed.

3

From 1954: Walcott, Clark, and the postcolonial

In the mid-twentieth century, the philosopher and psychiatrist Karl Jaspers posited 'tragic knowledge' as an 'achievement' which separates Western civilization from other cultures that have not reached such heights. He wrote:

> The greatest chasm separates those civilizations that never achieve tragic knowledge – and consequently its vehicles, tragedy, epic and the novel – from those whose way of life is determined by poignant awareness of the intrinsic part tragedy plays in man's existence. [...] The relaxed and serene face of the Chinese still contrasts with the tense and self-conscious expression of Western man.[1]

More recently, in 1990, the classicist Oliver Taplin argued that 'Greece is the geology underlying the mental landscape of Western civilization. The Greeks marked out the map of our conceptual geography and set the categories by which we order our perceptions'.[2] He contrasts this fundamental 'civilization' against multiple 'alien cultures'.[3]

In reaction, theatre scholar Kevin J. Wetmore Jr. writes that 'Taplin, and many other authors like him, see ancient Athens and its many cultural products (philosophy, democracy, tragedy, etc.) as unique, important, and at the center of western civilization'. But Wetmore cautions against eliding 'western' with 'universal', stating that 'We must remain wary of the idea that Greek tragedy is somehow "universal"'.[4] The literary critic Timothy J. Reiss expresses a similar suspicion about those who might apply ideas of the tragic to cultures that have developed away from the West, arguing that 'To denominate a culture and its members as tragic, its deeds and experiences as tragedy, replaces the local ambiguities of life and the realities of particular place and time, with someone else's overlaying transparency'.[5]

The anthropologist David Scott looks at a range of Western thinkers who have worried about the possibility of creating modern tragedy and writes, 'These are questions freighted with anguish, with doubt, and – not least, from my perspective – with *conceit*'. Scott perceives that thinkers such as Lukács, Williams, and Steiner tend to repeat, 'with wearisome unreflexiveness, a familiar story about the unique sources and character of Western civilization' and about how tragedy 'penetrates to the very heart of the human condition'.[6] Such scholars risk becoming the literary equivalent of the Western palaeontologists who once believed that dinosaurs of interest had predominantly resided in Europe and the United States because that was the scientists' backyard and primary area for their fossil digging. But does the study of tragedy necessitate this kind of viewpoint? Or is it possible to identify points of overlap and coincidence between tragic forms in places such as Western Europe and theatrical forms that have emerged in locations in, for example, the Global South, without the notion that one culture has become secondary to, or less significant than, the other?

The poet Derek Walcott is one whose work helps us to figure how we might consider the issues of tragedy in a postcolonial context. Walcott was born in January 1930 in Castries, the capital of Saint Lucia, in the West Indies. From about 1500, this mountainous island was colonized by the Western powers, and then repeatedly swapped hands between the British and French, with slaves of African heritage being imported from the

1720s to work the local coffee, cotton, and sugar plantations. The British gained formal possession in 1814 after suppressing a revolutionary party that was aided by slaves, and the colony finally achieved independence in 1979.[7] As a result of that history, Walcott grew up surrounded by an island culture which included both Anglophone and Francophone elements. According to Ingy Aboelazm, 'In his formative years, young Walcott perceived himself as much more like the whites than those darker and lower on the social scale, until in his teens he discovered the history of slavery, became conscious that his grandmothers were descended from slaves and experienced the discriminations of racial prejudice'.[8] Walcott began to script plays during the 1940s, at a point when the larger Caribbean islands had a reasonably well-developed culture of staging formal playhouse dramas, but which tended to be patronized and supported by the colonial class.[9] There did exist, however, a more popular set of performances that were manifested in carnivals and festivals, although these forms tended to exist quite separately from the drama being staged before the footlights. Walcott declared that, from his perspective, 'there was everything to be made'.[10] So he worked as a theatre maker, writer, and critic across the region, starting in his St Lucian home, then moving to Jamaica as a student, and then working with the Trinidad Theatre Workshop.[11]

One of Walcott's theatrical interventions was the one-act play, *The Sea at Dauphin*, which he wrote for a premiere in 1954 given by The New Company/The Whitehall Players, under the director of the dramatist Errol Hill (who also took the lead part of Afa). Hill had co-founded the company in 1946 in Trinidad and Tobago, with headquarters at Whitehall, Port-of-Spain.[12] Thus, although Walcott's play first appeared in Port-of-Spain, Trinidad, it was set in the village of Dauphin on Saint Lucia. As Walcott himself put it, '[e]very island in the Caribbean has its own syntactical structure: a Trinidadian is not going to understand a Jamaican the first time off'.[13] Indeed, the director of the original production commented that the drama was 'a little difficult for the non-St. Lucian', although the piece

was 'clarified for the spectator through dramatisation', and
Walcott subsequently revised the piece to make the dialogue
more widely accessible.[14] But just as Synge's use of Irish-
English had a political dimension in 1904, so in 1954 Walcott's
use of *patois*, the colloquial name for the version of French
with African elements that was spoken by people in St. Lucia,
showed that tragic drama might be articulated in the kind
of community where the language and identity of the people
had suffered from pejorative connotations. As the historians
Harmsen, Ellis, and Devaux point out, by the mid-twentieth
century, in the countryside of St. Lucia:

> the stigma of slavery had never quite been shaken off [...]
> farming continued to be associated to some extent with
> slavery, backwardness, *blue-black* African-ness, superstition,
> illiteracy and all things old-fashioned. The biggest mark of
> this alleged backwardness was rural people's inability to
> speak (or at least understand) English, the official language
> of St. Lucia.

As Harmsen, Ellis, and Devaux put it, *patois* was considered
unsophisticated 'despite the fact that virtually every St. Lucian
spoke it and, more importantly, enjoyed using it [...] English
had always been considered the language of the privileged, of
those who "*by virtue of education, occupation, and manner of
living*" did not rank in the same class as the common peasants,
labourers, artisans and fishermen'.[15] In *The Sea at Dauphin*,
then, Walcott reacted against such assumptions, showing that
the lives of fishermen whose version of English was strongly
inflected by *patois* were just as suitable to be the subject of tragic
drama as those whose language was associated with the white
community and the realm of banking, estate management, and
expensive sales.[16]

Derek Walcott's one-act play therefore revolves around two
fishermen who share possession of a boat. The first, Afa, is
a hardened forty-year-old bachelor. The second is a younger
man, Augustin, a less cynical figure, who wants his elderly

godfather Hounakin to come out and fish with them. When Afa was drunk, he invited Hounakin along, but now sees that the water is very rough and is displeased by Hounakin's tardy arrival at the shoreline. Hounakin has recently been widowed and is mourning his dead wife. Furthermore, Hounakin has never before been in a boat, and is petrified by the prospect. So the other two persuade him to stay on the shore, and he admits that he is caught in a bind. Hounakin is unable to beg because of his pride but he is also too tired to work, and so he remains hungry. Afa and Augustin agree to bring him some fish, but when they return they find he has committed suicide, with his body smashed to pieces on the rocks. A French priest attempts to console Afa, and the play ends as a young boy commences his own career as a fisherman.

When thinking about what had inspired this play, Walcott commented:

> I've always felt some kind of intimacy with the Irish poets because one realized that they were also colonials with the same kind of problems that existed in the Caribbean [...] When I read Synge's *Riders to the Sea* I realized [...] what he had attempted to do with the language of the Irish. He had taken a fishing-port kind of language and gotten beauty out of it, a beat, something lyrical. Now that was inspiring, and the obvious model for *The Sea at Dauphin*.[17]

Here, then, Walcott notes the similarity of situation that existed between Synge's Ireland and Saint Lucia. Both locations had a markedly Catholic heritage, with the laity manifesting considerable suspicion towards the clerical caste. In addition, both islands were strongly defined by their rural, agricultural surroundings. Walcott knew about Ireland because of the teachers and authors he encountered as a young man. 'When the Irish brothers came to teach at the college in St. Lucia, I had been reading a lot of Irish literature', Walcott reflected, 'I also sympathized with the most rebellious aspect of Irish literature, priest-hating and such. After all, I had seen the overwhelming surrender to superstition – not the church's superstition, but the power of French provincial priests in our island'.[18]

Walcott's *The Sea at Dauphin*, then, manifests many similarities with the tragedy written by Synge, with the very title of Walcott's work highlighting an affinity. At the end of *The Sea at Dauphin*, Afa mourns the dead and looks forward to his own demise:

Last year Annelles, and Bolo, and this year Hounakin ... And one day, tomorrow, you Gacia, and me ... And Augustin ... And we have only this shell for his old woman is in the *cimitière* behind the church, where Fond River coming down by the canes and making one with the sea at Dauphin ...[19]

This section of text adapts the words that Maurya speaks at the end of *Riders to the Sea*:

May the Almighty God have mercy on Bartley's soul, and on Michael's soul, and on the souls of Sheamus and Patch, and Stephen and Shawn [*bending her head*] ....and may He have mercy on my soul, Nora, and on the soul of everyone is left living in the world.[20]

One of the most discernible ways in which Synge influenced Walcott was in using dialect form to express tragic sentiment, and Walcott describes how this idea 'did come out of Synge'.[21] The Aran islanders of Synge's play speak a form of English that is strongly inflected by the syntax and grammar of the Irish language. Likewise, when Walcott came to write his play, he set it in Saint Lucia, where the most common creole has a French rather than an English lexicon. Hence the characters of Walcott's play often paraphrase their French creole phrases with English equivalents.

There is potentially a tension here. On the one hand, Walcott deployed a language in his play that resisted Western exploitation and celebrated local heritage. Yet on the other, Walcott used a theatrical form, that of tragedy, which is inherited from colonial Europe, leading Reiss to worry that, with this play, 'it will, precisely, be tragedy that guides the reader or spectator to how that history and its deformations are "properly" to be understood, western *ratio* imposing its "explanation" on a quite different culture'.[22]

Nonetheless, when writing *The Sea at Dauphin* Walcott did not simply reuse established notions of tragedy. Natalie Melas suggests using the term 'dissimilation' to allow for 'a mode of relation that does not depend on the recognition of sameness', and Michael Malouf suggests using a comparative model that allows the identification of the 'multiple relations' between texts.[23] Such an approach may steer us away from any simplistic view of measuring Walcott's work in terms of how much it borrows from Synge, and instead towards a cross-cultural reading that allows for moments of coincidence and recognition as well as difference and misrecognition. How might this work in practice? Well, let us take the overall tragic framework deployed by Synge and Walcott. Reiss identifies in Western culture a self-image that is embodied in tragedy. He argues that this self-image is 'riven with insuperable divides, scissions evinced as the essence of human life. Humans were split from the divine, other human groups, often each other, surely from the material world'.[24] This self-image means, as Reiss puts it, humans can only assume limited responsibility for the consequences of their actions: for example, Oedipus asserts 'It was Apollo, friends, Apollo,/ That brought this bitterness' and then asserts 'But the hand that struck me/ was none but my own'.[25] A modern version of this contradiction is found in Synge's *Riders to the Sea*, where Maurya worries that she has allowed her son to leave the house without giving him her blessing, and dashes to find him, with Cathleen admonishing her 'Isn't it sorrow enough is on everyone in this house without you sending him out with an unlucky word behind him [?]'.[26] After Maurya fails to bless Bartley, he dies. Yet the trajectory of her family's fate was already set before this: every one of her other sons had already been killed in similar circumstances, and the theological language of the play makes clear that the characters in the play understand how events happen 'by the grace of the Almighty'.[27]

As Reiss puts it, it is therefore 'basic to a modern Western sense of "self"' to see oneself as 'individually facing a greater divine, social, or political whole; indeed, facing-*off* with it in some more or less anguished conflict'.[28] Tragedy gives an aesthetic form to this sense of self, but it also delineates exactly who, and which peoples, are worthy of moral respect. Conveniently, tragedy often helps absolve Western cultures from various horrors inflicted around the globe. The Bengal famine, say, may have killed up to 3 million people, but applying the term 'tragic' potentially allows the situation to be described in terms of an Indian population facing natural forces and inevitable fate, rather than of deliberate colonial policies inflicted upon an agrarian economy. No-one is truly guilty or responsible for the overall catastrophe because these parameters are simply given, with tragic sentiment arising when people confront or make decisions within these parameters. Yet postcolonial drama may react against such aspects of Western thinking. In his study *Tragedy and Postcolonial Literature*, Ato Quayson argues that 'an idea of collective responsibility' is 'often foreclosed by the exclusive Western focus on individual agency', and he points instead to the way that familiar tragic concepts of *hamartia and anagnorisis* might be renegotiated through ideas such as those about the 'the disruption to the well-being of the community at large' held by the Akan people (one of the traditional matrilineal cultures of present-day Ghana/Ivory Coast).[29]

In Synge's play, we may discern something of what Reiss calls the 'usual Western view of the relation of "self" to, or *against*, divine, social, or some other totality'.[30] Maurya and her family are situated in anguish before an unyielding fate. After all, the reason why Maurya wants Bartley to stay at home in the first place is precisely because she has a premonition that he will be killed.[31] By the end of the play, Maurya apparently believes that events were determined from the start. Bad things happen because God has already decided that they must happen as part of His plan, which cannot be questioned because God is 'Almighty' and hence beyond human comprehension.[32] Maurya battles against this thinking earlier in the play, seeking to take the actions (such as belatedly hurrying to bless her son) that might ameliorate the situation, but by the end she arrives at acceptance. At the finish of the work she prays, 'Almighty God have mercy on Bartley's soul [...] No man at all can be living for ever, and we must be satisfied'.[33] Thus, the play does not end on a note of struggle against the almighty, but a weary and grief-stricken acceptance of fate: from which, naturally, audiences may dissent, but which they are certainly invited to share.

Walcott's *The Sea at Dauphin* works differently, and offers a contrast with the ideas of deity and fate that we find in Synge. In Walcott's play, Garcia, by commenting on the rough seas and poor fishing conditions, raises questions about the power of God. Garcia declares that 'God forget us' [i.e. God has forgotten us], revealing the deity to be, rather than omnipresent or all-powerful, instead a rather negligent entity.[34] The old man Hounakin demonstrates more respect for the divine than Garcia does, but still describes God as being distinctly human in characteristics, and by the end of the play Hounakin's faith that there is even a deity at all has disappeared. Before Hounakin commits suicide, he admits how, when his wife was dying and he was unable to afford medicine for her, he prayed, 'God you is old man like me, you put me here, I pray, I work', but his wife died nevertheless, and Hounakin concludes, 'I spit in the face of nothing./ You break your back for seventy cane reap times/ And then is ashes. A man cannot fight nothing, after all'.[35]

In the face of this negligent or absent God, Afa asks Augustin, 'What happen now? Gacia is God?', to which Augustin replies,

'No. You is God'.[36] Yimbu Emmanuel Nchia describes how, therefore, for the characters of Walcott's play:

God is not some supreme being but a fellow human. God to them becomes a metaphor for the person who is able to provide one's material needs and since, in the context of the play, God fails to relieve them from their hopelessness, they are obliged to consider each other as their own God.[37]

Walcott's play, then, resists straightforward comparison with the tragedy of *Riders to the Sea*. Indeed, Walcott's script presents the very language of fate and the deity as colonial relics, imposed by European empire-builders but having a questionable connection with daily life in the West Indies. As Afa declares:

God is a white man. The sky is his blue eye,
His spit on Dauphin people is the sea.
Don't ask me why a man must work so hard
To eat for worm to get more fat. Maybe I bewitch.
You never curse God, I curse him [...][38]

In Synge's *Riders to the Sea*, when Maurya is faced with religious authority, in the form of the 'young priest' who urges the people to trust in God, she demurs but scarcely moves towards any active resistance of the clerical message. Synge simply includes the following exchange:

Nora Didn't the young priest say the Almighty God wouldn't leave her destitute with no son living?

Maurya [*in a low voice, but clearly*].   It's little the like of him knows of the sea.[39]

Maurya's anger here is directed not towards God, but towards the priest. Some audience members may perceive that Maurya's philosophy has its limitations, but by the end of *Riders to the*

Sea, her faith in the deity has not been destroyed. Rather, her belief appears bolstered by the events that she has witnessed.[40]

However, a postcolonial articulation of tragedy may be situated in a different relationship to inherited cultural ideas and familiar traditions. *The Sea at Dauphin* portrays the church as an arm of the broader Western colonizing project, and so Walcott's play develops a more explicitly resistant commentary than that found in Synge's drama. Just as the denizens of Dauphin adapt the English language to suit their own circumstances and purposes, so they must adapt and attack various European concepts. When a young French priest attempts to offer words of comfort in the wake of Hounakin's suicide, Afa interrupts to declare:

> God! [*He turns and empties the fish pale on the sand*] That is God! A big fish eating small ones. And the sea, that thing there, not a priest white, pale like a shark belly we must feed until we dead, not no young Frenchman lock her up in a church don't know coolie man dying because he will not beg! [...] You see? Poverty, dirty women, dirty children, where all the prayers? [...] Where we have priest is poverty.[41]

Nirjhar Sarkar argues that, by contrast with the 'Resignation and defeat' that mark the end of Synge's *Riders to the Sea*, Walcott's *The Sea at Dauphin* reveals his characters 'being divested of illusions, they affirm the spirit of unwearied striving and self-overcoming'.[42] Hence the disparagement of the French priest speaks to a wider criticism of European colonialism, which has brought long-term poverty to the people of the island.

Overall, then, Walcott may have used the existing drama he knew from Synge, but has refused to provide audiences with some of the common European tragic structures that Synge deploys. Walcott himself said '*The Sea at Dauphin* is modeled completely on *Riders to the Sea*', and the colonial situation of the country of Ireland in which Synge and set the play may have felt resonant to Walcott.[43] As Quayson points out, the 'colonialized Other has been described in colonial discourse variously as black, dirty, lying, childlike, incapable of self-regulation, uncivilized, barbarian, effeminate, oversexed, etc', and Declan Kiberd is amongst the most influential critics to note that it is possible to recognize at least some of these tropes in imperial descriptions of the colonized Irish.[44] Yet Paul Breslin observes:

> In Walcott's account, the words 'mutating', 'translating', and 'retranslating' all point to the necessity of departing from what is already given – either in Synge's play or in St. Lucian speech – in order to write *The Sea at Dauphin*. Moving the setting from the Aran Islands to St. Lucia meant not only a change of language but a change of cultural milieu.[45]

Away from the Caribbean, similar questions about the remaking and reinvention of tragedy have also been raised by writers in very different postcolonial locations. The Nigerian poet J.P. Clark (known as John Pepper Clark-Bekederemo, and John Pepper Clark), also found inspiration in the work of J.M. Synge but sought to create tragedy that operates at variance with that of the established Western tradition. Both Clark and his fellow Nigerian playwright Wole Soyinka encountered Irish drama in the 1950s when studying as undergraduates at University College of Ibadan.[46] This university had been established in one of Nigeria's biggest cities during 1948, and during its first decade the institution admitted students such as Clark, Soyinka, and Chinua Achebe. This period marked a time of national cultural awakening in Nigeria, and chimed with the Irish literary revival that had happened half a century before, with the university's drama society producing plays including Synge's *The Playboy of the Western World*.[47] As Shyam S. Agarwalla puts it:

> In his last years in the Ibadan University, Clark had seen the performances of plays by J.M. Synge and W.B. Yeats. He had also read the playwrights as a part of his course.

Synge's interest in the tragic and comic aspects of Irish folk and Yeats's interest in Irish folklore influenced Clark that he was inspired to write *The Song of a Goat*.[48]

J.P. Clark arrived to study at Ibadan in 1955, having been born twenty years earlier in the Ijaw community of southeast Nigeria, the area of the Niger delta's mangrove swamps. As with Synge's Aran islanders, fishing had long been central to the life of this Nigerian population, with watermen specializing in sea fishing and often travelling far from home in order to work.[49] Siga Asanga writes that:

> apart from the occasional intrusion of the sirens of river-going steamers, Clark's Ijaw communities remain as isolated and equally as 'primitive' as were the Aran islanders of J.M. Synge at the end of the nineteenth century. The Ijaw country which Clark describes in his plays therefore is located on the west bank of the Niger river in outlets of the main Niger delta region, a fact which accounts, partially, for the predominance of isolated clusters of small settlements.[50]

Unsurprisingly, then, a number of critics have identified elements of Synge's tragic playwriting in the work of J.P. Clark, especially in Clark's first play *Song of a Goat*, which was published and performed in 1961, just a year after he left university.

Song of a Goat first appeared onstage, under Wole Soyinka's direction and with Soyinka playing the lead part of Zifa, in Ibadan, Nigeria, during 1961. As James Currey describes it, the Mbari Club where the work premiered was 'the Nigerian crossroads for everybody involved in the arts' with the stage being used for Nigerian-authored drama as well as for Yoruba travelling theatre and dance groups. For those involved, says Currey, 'Going beyond the classroom brought insights into African culture'.[51] During that two-week run of *Song of a Goat*, the play became a popular and critical success, then transferring to Lagos, Nigeria's biggest city, for another fortnight. Only after those performances did the play appear onstage in London. The play was also first published in Nigeria, and subsequently by Oxford University Press.

The story of *Song of a Goat* is relatively straightforward. It begins with the figure of the Masseur, who is 'crippled and itinerant' and is 'to many the family doctor, the confessor and the oracle'.[52] He is examining the female character of Ebiere, who has only had one child and has since been barren, a serious problem in a community where couples expect to have many children. She reveals that her husband, Zifa, an Ijaw fisherman, has been impotent since the time of her child's birth. The Masseur suggests that she should have sex with her husband's younger brother instead, in order to conceive a child. Ebiere rejects the offer, but the Masseur explains that it will be acceptable if the correct sacrifice is conducted. He tells her that she must 'Know the ways of our land' and offer a goat to 'the dead of/ The land'.[53] But Ebiere continues to refuse, and leaves in a state of great agitation. The Masseur then offers the same advice to her husband Zifa, who rejects the suggestion even more vehemently: this perhaps, in the terminology of Western hero-based tragedy, is his fatal flaw, an unwillingness to accept the solution that is sanctioned by tradition and by the gods.

Nonetheless, as the play continues, Zifa's younger brother does have sex with Ebiere, but they do not first conduct the correct sacrifice that would legitimize such an act. Zifa discovers what has happened, and angrily threatens to kill both his wife and his brother. Zifa sends his brother to fetch a goat, so that the ritual animal killing can belatedly be conducted, and then decapitates the beast. Zifa asks his wife to place the goat's head in a pot which then shatters, at which point she faints. Zifa now fetches his cutlass in order to murder his brother. However, a chorus of neighbours arrive to tell him some terrible news. His brother has already, filled with shame, hanged himself with his loin cloth. Zifa realizes that he has destroyed his family and his brother's life, and the audience learns that Ebiere has miscarried. In the final lines of the play, Zifa drowns himself.

Song of a Goat appeared at a moment of political change and uncertainty in J.P. Clark's homeland. The area now known as Nigeria had been colonized by the British Empire during the nineteenth century, but in 1929 the effects of global depression meant the people found colonial rule increasingly intolerable, and anti-colonial activists worked hard to guarantee the complete liberation of the country. Eventually Nigeria declared independence in 1960, and *Song of a Goat* appeared the following year (the country became a republic in 1963 and then fell to a coup in 1966, with military governments holding sway until the restoration of democracy in 1999).[54] Theatre scholarship often describes Clark and Soyinka as part of a 'first generation' of Nigerian playwrights who pursued their art from about 1960 and often used European tragic forms in conjunction with Nigerian ideas. For example, as Osita Okagbue puts it, these writers created work containing 'an essentially tragic vision and an aesthetic of cultural retrieval [...] For Soyinka, as well as for the others, life is an endless cycle of mistakes repeated through generations and it is futile trying to break out of this cycle', rather like the philosophy of Synge's Maurya.[55] One of those who knew both Clark and Soyinka, the scholar Bruce King, writes that this was the first generation to go to university in Nigeria and that it enabled Nigerian literature to reach 'the point of what economists call "take off"'. King argues that 'The students had a traditional African culture marginally around them but their actual, primary culture, was Western, British'. Figures like Clark and Soyinka certainly knew about British culture from the school and university classroom, as well as from university cultural activities such as dance clubs, choirs, drama groups; and 'Basically the Nigerians wrote in relationship to the European literature tradition as taught to them by the British'.[56] However, this group also became concerned with:

> the infusion of the local, in this case a re-Africanisation. At first it was mostly a matter of theme, subject matter, and concern with the role of European languages in Africa, but

soon the Ibadan group was asking how they could make use
of oral literature, ritual, myth, belief, and of new popular
forms that had developed at the intersection of the West
and Africa.[57]

David Scott has made the argument that decolonization
might provide a moment that is 'especially conducive to
tragic consciousness'.[58] To make his case, Scott draws on
Albert Camus' ideas from the 1955 lecture 'On the Future
of Tragedy', in which Camus asserted that 'great periods of
tragic art occur, in history, in centuries of crucial change, at
moments when the life of peoples is heavy both with glory
and with threats, when the future is uncertain and the present
dramatic'.[59] Camus saw that at such historical junctures, there
is a lack of certainty: one traditional structure may have ebbed
away, but has yet to be fully or properly replaced. Camus, of
course, viewed this historical process through a thoroughly
Eurocentric lens, looking for tragic theatre solely in 'the thirty
centuries of Western history'.[60] He identified ancient Greece
and the early modern world of Shakespeare as providing
true tragic moments, when man 'frees himself from an older
form of civilization and finds that he has broken away from
it without having found a new form which satisfies him'.[61]
Camus wondered whether his own era, which was dominated,
in France at least, by the war of 1939–45 and by the outbreak
of the decolonizing Algerian War from 1954, might provide
another period that would allow another resurgence of tragedy,
and Scott builds on Camus's idea by arguing that 'the making
and the unmaking of modern colonial worlds are exemplary of
moments of great historical rupture'.[62]

Synge had created *Riders to the Sea* at a moment in Irish
history when a nationalist movement was moving towards
rebellion, warfare, and the governmental independence of most
of the island in 1922. So the project for Synge and his fellow
national-theatre directors was to articulate the distinctiveness
of Irish culture, from which political disaggregation might
logically follow. Likewise, Clark's *Song of a Goat* appeared

in the year after Nigerian independence, at a stage when a distinctive Ijaw culture might be shown onstage but when the overall nation and its polity remained in flux.

As Clark's friend Wole Soyinka has emphasized, Clark was not simply replicating a pre-existing Western mode of tragic thought. In the important study *Myth, Literature and the African World*, Soyinka explains that *Song of a Goat* might relate to the 'haunting habitations of John Synge'.[63] Soyinka observes that, in *Song of a Goat*, 'We encounter human beings whose occupation and environment are elemental and visceral. Flood and ebb affect their daily existence, their language, their spectrum of perception'.[64] The end of *Song of a Goat* is the moment when Clark's play most closely echoes that of Synge, as Zifa's death mirrors that of Bartley's in *Riders to the Sea*. When Bartley dies in Synge's play, it is the day of the fair when Bartley has gone to sell his horse: Nora and Cathleen hear 'someone after crying out by the seashore', only to learn, moments later, that he has been 'knocked [...] into the sea, and he was washed out where there is a great surf'.[65] When Zifa dies in *Song of a Goat*, it is market day, the neighbours see him 'reach the water's edge' before 'he bellowed' at the ocean, and then 'waded into the deep/ As one again in sleep'.[66] However, Soyinka indicates that *Riders to the Sea* has a more arbitrary collection of tragic ideas, implying that Clark did a better job than Synge in resolving those elements: 'The poetic containment of violence is very much the environmental reality of *Song of a Goat*. Storms do not occur every day nor are fishermen washed off their canoes on every fishing-trip'.[67]

The titular goat in *Song of a Goat* illustrates that Clark may have been looking towards the traditions of established Western tragedy whilst, at the same time, creating a form of the tragic that articulated, in Soyinka's terms, a different 'spectrum of perception'. In fact, the goat became deeply problematic at the premiere at the Mbari Club in Ibadan. The live animal was decapitated *for real* during the first performance, but Martin Banham describes how 'without adequate rehearsal' this act became a 'chastening experience' when more than a 'single stroke' was required to kill the animal.[68] After that first performance, the performed sacrifice became symbolic rather than literal, although Wole Soyinka described how the goat continued to pose problems. When staged in London, 'A rather lively goat [...] tended to punctuate passages of intended solemnity with bleats from one end and something else from the other'.[69] But what was the goat doing there at all? As already noted, the etymological roots of 'tragedy' are in those Greek words *tragos* ('goat') and *oidos* ('song'). In addition to that European legacy, Clark may have intended *Song of a Goat* to recall African ritual sacrifice. Wetmore points out that 'Clark was attempting to resacralize drama, to add a real sacrificial ritual to the onstage action so that the play transcended mere drama and became a genuine communal tragedy'.[70]

Thus *Song of a Goat* may point to traditional ideas about European tragedy, but also to ideas that are indigenous to particular places in Africa. John Povey emphasizes that the words of Clark's play echo 'the old mother of Synge's *Riders to the Sea*'.[71] Povey highlights a specific point of similarity in the moment at which the main female character in *Song of a Goat*, the aunt, laments the misfortunes that have affected her family:

> There will never be light again in this
> House, child, this is the night of our race,
> The fall of all that ever reared up head
> Or crest.[72]

However, Povey points out that the key difference between this lament and that of *Riders to the Sea* is that, in *Song of a Goat*, the mourner then 'turns to her Africa for the clinching image', with Povey quoting the aunt's lines 'White ants/ have passed their dung on our roof-top./ Like a tree rotten in the rain, it/ Topples'.[73] The ideas of mourning that we might find in Synge's work, then, are combined here with a depiction of the distinctive environment of the Ijaw people.

At times, Clark's *Song of a Goat* explicitly calls to mind a number of Western tragic precedents. There are a number of self-conscious allusions to Shakespearean tragedy: for instance, as King Lear on the heath yelled 'Blow, winds, and crack your cheeks! rage! blow', so the suicidal Zifa in Clark's play responds to the noise of the large boats on the sea shore by yelling: 'Blow,/ Blow, sirens, blow […] blow till your hooting drown/ the moaning of the sea'.[74] Other features of *Song of a Goat* resonate with the broader ideas of European tragedy. For one thing, tragedy often contains the idea of a familial curse (Oedipus and Antigone, for example, are doomed because they belong to the house of Labdacus; Romeo and Juliet because of the feuding Montagues and Capulets). In *Song of a Goat*, Zifa neglects the correct procedures for sacred rites and honouring ancestors, repeats the mistakes of his own father, and is told of 'this curse upon your head'.[75]

A number of critics have pointed to this recycling of familiar tragic ideas in Clark's play. James Ndukaku Amankulor, for example, suggests that the prophetic aunt in *Song of a Goat* 'may be a dramatic counterpart of Tiresias', whilst Martin Owusu notes that the drama 'illustrates the Greek convention of avoiding violent death on stage'.[76] Clark himself wrote a revised ending to *Song of a Goat*, which brings it still closer towards the ideas of Greek tragedy. In the 'alternative close', the Masseur would finish the play by pointing to the role of fate, declaring: 'This was no fire begun/ By ordinary hand. All fire comes/ From God'.[77] The Masseur then offers the concluding advice:

Do not, my people, venture overmuch
Else in unravelling the knot, you
Entangle yourselves. It is enough
You know now that each day we live
Hints at why we cried out at birth.[78]

Clark's revised ending echoes the mood and sentiment that ends Sophocles' *Oedipus Rex*, which concludes with the line 'Count no mortal happy till he has passed the final limit of his life secure from pain'.[79] Clark himself acknowledged that 'It is quite possible that Sophocles and Euripides are in that play'.[80]

At another moment, Clark described the main character in *Song of a Goat* as 'surely' demonstrating 'tragic passion as the Greeks knew it'.[81]

However, Clark also wrote, in *The Example of Shakespeare*, that it would be wrong to view echoes in form, theme, or structure as necessarily indicating any simplistic notion of cultural borrowing and debt. As he put it:

> The implication is not that one group of people borrowed this and that property from another but that there can and do occur areas of coincidence and correspondence in the way of living among several peoples separated by vast distances and time, and who apparently are of distinct cultures, practices, and persuasions. For example, the orchestra and leader-chorus arrangement of characters occupies as much a principal part in Nigerian theatre as it did in Greek theatre. But this is not to say one is debtor to the other. It is a matter of correspondence and coincidence.[82]

Clark himself saw strong parallels between the way in which Nigerian performance had developed, and the way in which he saw that Western drama had evolved from chanting, music, and ritual movement. Clark wrote that 'We believe that as the roots of European drama go back to the Egyptian Osiris and the Greek Dionysus so are the origins of Nigerian drama likely to be found in the early religious and magical ceremonies and festivals of the peoples of this country'.[83]

Clark declared that he came from 'ancient multiple stock in the Niger delta area of Nigeria from which I have never quite felt myself severed', and the unique nature of that region allowed him to develop a form that might coincide with Western tragedy but in other respects looks quite different from that long seen on the European stage.[84] As T.O. McLoughlin puts it:

> The repeated locale of his [Clark's] plays, the river delta area, confirms this sense of rootedness in the sensuous, social, cultural and mythological character of a particular place. Most of his characters take their livelihood from the

river and the sea. In his work the tides, the creeks, the ships, ports, fog have a teasing fascination: sometimes they are symbolic of loneliness, chaos and death, but always they are firm images of a particular people and their way of life.[85]

Some of these features could, of course, also be noted in the work of Synge. Yet there are aspects of *Song of a Goat* that look deeply unfamiliar when viewed from the perspective of the Western tragic imagination, especially in the central subject matter of Clark's play. In the West, sexual impotence is not conventionally considered a subject for tragedy. Indeed, impotence is more usually considered as material for comedy. Problematic sexual relationships have long been part of European conceptions of tragedy (Agamemnon and Clytemnestra, say, or Othello and Desdemona) and Zifa's feelings about his wife and brother seem to carry something of this implication, as he threatens murderous retribution against his brother. But incapacity has never really been part of the range of sexual problems thought to have a tragic implication on the European stage. For example, J.M. Synge presents the image of the impotent man (whose wife complains was 'always cold, every day since I knew him, – and every night') but Synge includes this character in the comic drama, *In The Shadow of the Glen*, which concludes not with death but with the wife escaping from her husband for a liberated life with a tramp.[86]

Hence, when the British-based theatre critic Martin Esslin examined *Song of a Goat*, he felt that this central subject matter completely disqualified Clark's play from being categorized as tragic. As Esslin wrote: 'The motivation of the tragedy, which is simply the husband's inability to engender a child, is far too simple and unoriginal to support the weight of full-scale tragedy across the generations'.[87]

However, Peter Benson responded to Esslin by writing:

The 'husband's inability to engender a child' is 'too simple and unoriginal to support the weight of full-scale tragedy'? In *Africa*, where parenthood is more important than wealth, and impotence is a calamity beyond naming?

Esslin's ruminations simply show that his 'quite differently conditioned feelings' were precisely what made it impossible for him to judge.[88]

There is clearly a danger here of essentializing 'Africa', an enormous continent of widely different peoples, customs, landscapes, cultures, and nations. But despite the unfortunate way in which Benson stated his case, his broad argument was endorsed by Wole Soyinka, who agreed that Clark's play typified a more general gulf between European and African responses to *Song of a Goat*. Soyinka declares that 'unlike some African audiences before whom this play has since been staged, the European audience found itself estranged from the tragic statement', with Soyinka pointing out that one of reasons might be 'the essential divergences of the European cast of mind from the African'. Some African audiences might recognize, rather than simply the discrete agonies of one person, the way this pain reflected a rupture in the communal psyche. European audiences, felt Soyinka, found the subject matter of *Song of a Goat* 'outside the range of tragic dimensions' because 'sexual impotence was a curable condition in modern medicine' and because 'child adoption provided one remedy, among others, for sterility'. Such thinking led Soyinka to wonder, along the lines of Brecht, about whether other dramas could truly be considered tragic for Europeans. If syphilis – the inherited, sexually transmitted disease around which Ibsen's *Ghosts* revolves – was no longer incurable, then perhaps Ibsen's play had lost the tragic rationale it may once have had.[89] Ultimately, Soyinka contrasts African and European drama as 'representative of the essential differences between two world-views, a difference between one culture [the African] whose very artefacts are evidence of a cohesive understanding of irreducible truths and another [the European], whose creative impulses are directed by period dialectics'.[90]

Wetmore finds that it is by 'using Greek form to explore an African tragic theme [that] Clark develops a uniquely African tragedy'.[91] He argues that Clark's plays 'generate meaning by rejecting Eurocentrist interpretation and indigenous explanation, and rather explore the modern African experience through a hybrid of classical Europe and contemporary Africa'.[92] The production of such drama is a response to European territorial conquest, with some African writers potentially engaging in a form of cultural resistance to Western hegemony. *Song of a Goat* may not directly address the colonial situation and its injustices, but in producing a drama that revolves entirely around characters who are Ijaw, Clark is demonstrating the theatrical validity of the specifically located lives and experiences that creators of tragic theatre had long ignored. As Wetmore puts it, such 'intercultural' or 'post-Afrocentric' writing 'does not automatically challenge and refute all things Western, but rather explores the complex relationship between Afroculture and Euroculture'.[93] As he puts it:

> J.P. Clark developed a hybrid tragedy. He used Greek form and structure, including the illustration of the *hamartia* in the case of Zifa, followed by a recognition and reversal. The *hamartia* concept finds a correlation in the Ijaw belief of the Agreement between a *teme* [soul] and the creator. By his use of a series of rituals [...] Clark also connected his tragedy to the origins of tragedy in ritual sacrifice. He placed the story in an African setting, used African subject matter, and ensured that his characters' actions were appropriate and believable within an African context, regardless of Greek conceptualization of those actions. Clark has transcultured Greek form and structure through the Ijaw world-view into an African context, creating a truly African tragedy and true transcultural artefact.[94]

Likewise, Osita Okagbue argues that 'In spite of this closeness to Greek models, Clark portrays life in his delta Ijo homeland as he knows it. Each play therefore deals with an aspect of life that is important to Ijo people – traditional practices, like marriage and procreation, and socioeconomic practices, like fishing, trading, and lumbering'.[95] However, Wetmore and

Okagbue's view is scarcely uncontested. Douglas Killam and Alicia Kerfoot, for instance, have asserted that *Song of a Goat* play is straightforwardly 'a tragedy in the Greek classical mode'.[96]

Timothy J. Reiss's interpretation falls somewhere in the middle of these divergent views. As Reiss sees it, Clark's play offers a point of triangulation between two other kinds of tragic drama. One type is a straightforward African adaptation of an existing tragic play, such as Wole Soyinka's *Bacchae*. The other type is a play that appears to be tragic but actually has no direct reference outside African culture, such as Ama Ata Aidoo's *Anowa*, Ebrahim Hussein's *Kinjeketile*, and Sony Labour Tansi's *La parenthèse de sang* ('Parentheses of Blood'). Clark's *Song of a Goat* sits between these two: it is not a direct adaptation of an earlier European tragedy, but does contain reminders of classical tragedy in an entirely Ijaw setting.[97]

The reasons why such debates have become vexed may be, in part, because there is obviously a danger here. Given the violent appropriations and continuing biases of colonialism, a comparison with any earlier European work risks diminishing the significance of African art. If we only view *Song of a Goat* in the light of *Riders to the Sea* and Western tragic precursors, then the power and originality of Clark's play may be lost. There is, after all, barely any correlation in plot between Clark and Synge's work. Yet, when *Song of a Goat* first appeared in Britain, alongside work by Wole Soyinka, as part of a Commonwealth Arts Festival in 1965, the theatre reviewer in the *Observer*, Penelope Gilliat, wrote that:

> Every decade or so, it seems to fall to a non-English dramatist to belt new energy into the English tongue. The last time was when Brendan Behan's 'The Quare Fellow' opened [... Now] a Nigerian called Wole Soyinka has done for our napping language what brigand dramatists from Ireland have done for centuries: booted it awake, rifled its pockets and scattered the loot into the middle of next week.[98]

Quite aside from the disturbing association of the peoples of Ireland and Nigeria with violence and crime ('brigand dramatists'? 'belt'? 'booted it awake, rifled its pockets'?), there is an immense condescension here. It appears that postcolonial cultures exist on the periphery, of little interest in their own right, and mainly of concern insofar as to how they might periodically contribute to revivifying a theatrical life that remains at a notional centre. Meanwhile, *The Times* reviewed the same performances in 1965, and commented that 'Compared with Mr. Soyinka's urban drama, with its delectable western influence, Mr. Clark's plays are wholly indigenous and defiantly unsophisticated'.[99] For *The Times*, then, a deviation from Western theatrical traditions is a removal from the realm of the 'delectable' into something altogether 'unsophisticated'.

Some critics have questioned the appropriateness for non-Western writers of using Western notions of tragedy in the first place, as the very concept of the tragic is freighted with historically problematic ideas. Marianne McDonald, for example, points to the danger of 'culturally imperialistic propaganda [that] establishes who ought to rule and who is meant to be ruled', and highlights the fact that Aristotle himself 'articulated the philosophy that nature determines who is a ruler and who a slave'.[100] As Biodun Jeyifo notes, the danger is that, 'what we routinely encounter is that no matter how strongly they call for an indigenous tragic art form, our authors smuggle into their dramas, through the back door of formalistic and ideological predilections typically conventional Western notions and practices of rendering historical events into tragedy'.[101]

Indeed, theatre makers in postcolonial contexts can attract stern criticism for moving their work too closely towards pre-existing notions of tragedy. For example, when the South African playwright of European descent, Athol Fugard, wrote his first play, the 1956 work *Klaas and the Devil*, he admitted to modelling the piece 'on Synge's *Riders to the Sea* because it expressed so well the concerns of the township [...] what was happening on stage was in fact a reflection of and a comment on our own lives'.[102] Fugard's play was, as he describes it, 'very much like JM Synge's The [*sic*] Riders to the Sea, that wonderful Irish play. Very much about fishing folk, an arrogant fisherman and the devil'.[103] Unfortunately that work by Fugard is no longer extant, but when he subsequently co-created a play about South African racial injustice (*The Island*, 1973), he once again attempted to utilize two other European models, *Antigone* and *Waiting for Godot*. This use of such dramas prompted Robert Mshengu Kavanagh to urge Fugard, to 'turn his attention away from London, Paris and New York to the cultural and dramatic activity of the majority in his own country and throughout the world'.[104] Errol Durbach highlights a Marxist critique of Fugard that asks:

> [Why] does he not inveigh against the exploitative nature of capitalism in South Africa? Why does he accept the situation as unalterable instead of agitating for change? Why does he not immerse himself more sympathetically in the culture and languages of the black proletariat? Why does he not draw upon indigenous African traditions and myths for his plays?[105]

Nonetheless, it is possible to construct an alternative argument, and I want to conclude this chapter by highlighting how critical and theatrical interventions focused on Nigeria may draw on established Western notions of tragedy, whilst at the same time redefining those notions of tragedy. These interventions show how the tragic might be suitable for understanding particular local postcolonial circumstances, in ways that speak to an emergent set of political and environmental challenges.

In his 2003 volume, *Calibrations*, Ato Quayson makes the case for why tragedy might be suitable for depicting and comprehending real-life Nigeria. He looks at the writer and minority-rights activist Ken Saro-Wiwa, who drew public attention to the degradation of the Niger delta by oil companies, notably Royal Dutch Shell, and was hanged by the Nigerian government in 1995. Quayson utilizes tragic theory, particularly that of Aristotle, in order to describe Saro-Wiwa's heroism, and recommends drawing on 'certain specific literary paradigms, such as tragedy, as they provide tools by which to analyse political actions at the dual levels of structure and agency'. In this way, Quayson argues, we might 'calibrate the literary paradigm to help further our understanding of process, change, and contradiction in a slice of postcolonial history'.[106] For Quayson, then, the terms and concepts of Aristotelian tragedy may function, not only as an alien imposition, but as a way of accessing and understanding the particularities of this postcolonial situation.

Quayson promotes the idea of 'link[ing] the seriousness and rigor with which literary tragedy is often dealt – its aesthetic, emotional, philosophical, ethical, and formal intensities – to an engagement with a specific event or set of events in the world'.[107] Indeed, it might be possible to deploy the critical approach that Quayson advocates in order to help understand certain injustices faced by Nigeria in the years since J.P. Clark wrote *Song of a Goat*. Clark created his play in 1961, shortly before oil exploration began in earnest in the Niger delta. Hence, oil is not mentioned in his play at all. But since that time, the major petroleum companies and their partner organizations have shown a brutal willingness to pursue profit at the cost of the environment of that part of Nigeria, and also at the cost of the health and wellbeing of those who live there.

Today, then, those who live in the Niger delta face death and destruction as a result of an exploitative, neo-colonial enterprise. The Nigerian Oil Spill Monitor recorded more than 6,600 spills between 2005 and 2015 alone.[108] Best Ordinioha and Seiyefa Brisibe report that an average of 240,000 barrels of crude oil are spilled in the Niger delta each year; an Aristotelian *hamartia* that spreads carcinogens and radioactive materials into the surrounding areas. These incidents lead to a horrifying *peripeteia*: an estimated 60 per cent reduction in household food security, a 24 per cent increase in childhood malnutrition, and a significant risk of infertility and cancer. Such systematic corporate carelessness, in which 'accidents' are integral to the programme and thus entirely fated within an overall established structure, has thus introduced a slow poison into the landscape, and the *pathos* of a silent spring where the toxins take years to bring about illness and death.[109] Just as the characters of Synge's *Riders to the Sea* or Sophocles' *Oedipus Rex* were doomed from the start, so children who are born within 10 km of an oil spill, even one that took place five years before their conception, face an enormously increased likelihood of early death. Perhaps we should not be surprised that when Anna Bruederle and Roland Hodler wrote a scientific paper on this cause and effect they described the situation as an 'ongoing human tragedy'.[110]

Greg Mbajiorgu addresses these issues in his three-act play, *Wake Up Everyone*, which was first developed as a short experimental piece in the Nicon Luxury Hotel, Abuja in 2009, and then staged in abbreviated form at the University of Nigeria, Nsukka, in 2011. The play is set in the fictional Nigerian community of Ndoli, which has witnessed the sudden arrival of oil wealth. In the play, the local-government chairman is a figure who, at one time, had joined a militant group and combated the oil companies that despoiled the local land. However, after one colossal oil spillage ruined the area of Ndele village, and killed his own father, the chairman spied an opportunity. He threatened legal action against the oil companies, and in response they agreed to bankroll his bid to become chairman of the Ndoli government on the secret understanding that he would cease to work on behalf of the surrounding farmers. In one of the most resonant scenes of the play, we see a recreation of the chairman's campaign speeches in which he promises political action whilst inwardly knowing that he will do nothing to help the nearby people and environment.

Mbajiorgu's play thus makes the case that the multinational oil companies bring about a moral as well as a literal pollution of the Nigerian landscape. They ruin the delta environment through spillages, and, through their patronage of local political figures, compromise those leaders and make it impossible for such politicians to act. Characters do say 'I thank God' and 'by the gods'.[111] But the environment in which they live is not being ravaged by any deity, but by the fact that 'man has made the world to be in its present bad state [...] he continues this rape of the planet'.[112] The characters repeatedly refer to the 'tragedy' of their situation, but tragedy here lies not in the downfall of one figure, but in the manmade downfall of the whole community and its surrounding ecosystem.[113] As one character declares, 'People of our land, that is man's ordeal for you. Humanity's brutal and outrageous quest for wealth and development has nothing but the promise of doom and poverty for the children's generation'.[114]

In *Wake Up Everyone*, we may find echoes of J.M. Synge, Derek Walcott, and J.P. Clark, all of whose plays focused on fishing, drowning, and the sea. Mbajiorgu's play presents the sympathetic figure of Professor Madukwe Aladinma, who educates others about climate change and environmental protection, urges an attentiveness to the local surroundings, and points out that 'Ndoli land as you know, is a coastal region and like all coastal areas, its closeness to the sea makes it prone to flooding as the rivers easily overflow their banks'.[115] The other characters repeatedly refer to the sea, and by the play's conclusion, spectators are confronted by loud noise and screams as the predicted flood finally arrives, destroying all the crops of the local farmlands. One character predicts that even worse will follow in the future: 'when a serious natural disaster hits a major coastal city like Lagos where most of the lands were reclaimed from water'.[116]

At times, the play features a fatalism about such events (the worst tragedy of all 'will' occur).[117] Yet within this overall vision of inevitable destruction, Mbajiorgu's play allows for a Brechtian possibility of change. The professor concludes the play by declaring: 'The earth is dying, dragging all in it to its grave'. But he then continues, 'We've got to cure it of its sickness. This is the time to save it, after all, we made it sick in the first place'.[118] At the end of Brecht's *Señora Carrar's Rifles*, as noted in the previous chapter, we find the main character concluding the play by raising her gun in order to fight fascism. Likewise, at the end of *Wake Up Everyone* we find the local people of Ndoliland driven to take violent measures: '*One of the farmers raises a song of protest, everyone joins as they brandish their farm machetes and diggers and move towards the Local Government Chairman's residence*'.[119] The professor is clear that he favours education and research, but he realizes that the situation has evolved to the point that others will take more extreme actions to achieve change. The implicit question to the audience at the play's conclusion is this: what will you do in order to avert the coming crisis?

We began this chapter by thinking about the dangers of tragic thinking. As David Scott puts it, tragedy often tends, with 'wearisome unreflexiveness', to deliver 'a familiar story about the unique sources and character of Western civilization'.[120] But Ato Quayson makes the case that by viewing particular elements of postcolonial society through the lens of tragedy it might be possible to arouse 'people into engagement with their history'.[121] By the time we reach the work of Greg Mbajiorgu in 2011, and his drama of the collective downfall of a Nigerian community through ecological despoilment, we find a play derived from the uniqueness of Nigeria's own politics and environment, and a play that nonetheless manifests a number of coincidences and correspondences with the earlier notions of tragedy that have been discussed in this volume. Thus, Mbajiorgu is able to articulate something that might be both culturally distinctive to the postcolonial situation and socially urgent well beyond Nigeria. Such an individuated articulation of the form may play through into a broader encouragement for those who have been marginalized to speak of their own experience and their own predicament, and shows how engagement with varieties of tragic thinking may be used to *Wake Up Everyone*.

Conclusion

Theatrical ideas about tragedy have changed over time, have shifted in the light of ongoing political concerns, and, as we have seen in this volume, have often been reappraised from an array of varying social and cultural perspectives. In pre-independence Ireland, J.M. Synge developed a Nietzschean aspect to the tragedy of *Riders to the Sea*, and, in response to the Spanish Civil War and the Second World War, Brecht drew on Hegel and Marx to create tragedies of political immediacy in *Señora Carrar's Rifles* and *Antigone*. Subsequently, in the post-war era, Derek Walcott and J.P. Clark again looked back to Synge, creating new plays that situate tragic action in postcolonial contexts and which disrupt pre-existing notions of fate, the heroic individual, and the deity.

There are, of course, a number of other shifting ideas about modern tragedy that we have not had space to discuss in this slim volume, and an important one of these ideas is the way in which notions of theatrical tragedy might relate to ideas of gender. Given the restrictions of word count here, I have struggled to incorporate adequate discussion of this important topic, but, in this concluding section, I did wish to highlight a few points about gender and tragedy. It can certainly be argued that the plays that we have examined in this book display a regressive view of male-female relationships. In J.M. Synge's *Riders to the Sea*, for example, a woman is the central character of the drama, but she and the play's other women have an entirely domestic role. It is a woman's job to prepare bread, mend clothes, and mourn the dead. By contrast, the men have a more active societal function outside the home. It is men who can sell horses and travel across the sea. Synge's work may be observing a reality on the Aran islands at that time, but his play was scarcely in the vanguard of challenging such gendered roles. Similarly, with Brecht's *Señora Carrar's Rifles*, the main character has the name Teresa Carrar, but throughout the printed script her character is labelled 'The mother' before each occasion that the character speaks. None of the male characters are linked with their parental role in this way, and so, in rehearsal, this potentially encourages actors to emphasize a set of essentialised social attitudes.

In J.P. Clark's *Song of a Goat*, we find the characters expressing misogyny quite directly. The impotent Zifa, for example, refers to Ebiere's womb in territorial terms by saying 'I will not give up my piece of land'.[1] Women in that play are repeatedly labelled with a derogatory language of insanity. Ebiere is told, 'Why, Ebiere, you are mad', shortly before she admits that 'I am crazed', whilst the only other female character, Orukorere, is described in the *dramatis personae* as 'half-possessed'.[2] Similarly, in Derek Walcott's *The Sea at Dauphin*, the men are clearly individuated, but the female characters appear *en masse* as a chorus and, where they do speak individual lines, are labelled with titles such as 'first woman', 'a woman', or 'another'. As Michael Malouf points out, in *The Sea at Dauphin*, 'the women reveal no argument or perspective of their own but rather only express the repressed feelings of the male characters'.[3] Furthermore, both Walcott and Brecht have been the subject of well-publicised controversies about their mistreatment of women in real life, and those revelations have undoubtedly tarnished the reputation of both dramatists, causing scholars (not least the author of the present volume) to worry about the appropriate presentation of work by these playwrights.[4]

Still, in response to male-focused theatrical tragedies, female playwrights have increasingly sought to reframe the themes and tropes of the form, and to react against those patriarchal impulses. Zinnie Harris, Marina Carr, and Suzan-Lori Parks, for example, are amongst the prominent female theatre makers who have taken the characters and themes of the tragic canon and reinvented those ideas in new contexts. Sarah Kane is perhaps the best known of such figures, with her work repeatedly including a set of recognizable ideas from Attic and Early Modern tragedy. For example, the eye-gouging of *Blasted* (1995) and the moment when one character injects heroin into the eyeball of another in *Cleansed* (1998) both connect with the blinding of Oedipus, and that of Gloucester in *King Lear*. Her play *Phaedra's Love* (1996) likewise points back to the Roman tragedy of Seneca. Elsewhere, the torture and dismemberment of Carl in *Cleansed*, and the death of the child at the end of *Blasted*, offer a reminder of *Medea*, and one of the great losses of world theatre is the version of Euripides' play that Kane was planning to create at the time of her early death.[5]

There are some clear reasons why writers such as Kane may have wished to revisit and revise the established realm of tragedy. Many of the key tragic texts include assumptions that are deeply regressive. A heteronormative set of ideas, for instance, tends to underpin important parts of the Western tragic canon. There is, similarly, an ableist bias in many of those texts. Philoctetes, for example, is lamed by a foul-smelling ulcer, Hamlet and Lear apparently suffer from mental illness, while Oedipus must lose his sight and bears a name that means 'swollen ankle'. Such prejudice has, in recent years, been challenged by actors in the British Graeae theatre company, whilst other groups have likewise wished to question the self-evident ageism, sexism, and racism that are found in many of the core tragic plays that have been perceived to articulate a 'universal' human experience.[6]

The postcolonial dramatists Derek Walcott and P.J. Clark, as discussed in the final chapter, worked to overcome the old imperial, Eurocentric ideas that have long been inherent in tragedy. But there is always a danger that a new set of hierarchies and biases are established, perhaps excluding female, queer, elderly, trans, disabled, and many other voices. Theatre makers with varying social perspectives and from a range of cultural traditions may sometimes find, therefore, that the cultural and intellectual baggage of tragedy makes the form an uncongenial one.

However, as this book has attempted to demonstrate, modern tragedy has repeatedly been shaped by theatre makers who overthrow existing assumptions about the form, and innovation has happened through modification or sometimes deeply hostile reaction to earlier examples and norms. As this volume has noted, Brecht wrote tragedy whilst wishing to demolish many of the influential assumptions that derived from Aristotle. Later in the twentieth century, when Wole Soyinka wrote his 1968 essay 'The Fourth Stage' he thought about the tragic by using his knowledge of Nietzsche, as well as his awareness of the terminology of G. Wilson Knight (his professor at Leeds University), whilst at the same time drawing on his knowledge of Yoruba traditions from Nigeria. Soyinka was therefore able to compare and contrast sensibilities that were tragic or coincided with tragedy, seeing the Yoruba god of iron and war, Ogun, as 'a totality of the Dionysian, Apollonian and Promethean virtues'.[7] Soyinka, then, remained sensitive to the parallels existing between the Greek tragedy and Yoruba belief, but he did not wish to allow established notions of European tragedy to overwhelm the Nigerian dimension.

Ultimately, then, Soyinka shows that it is possible to be aware of the problematic history of tragic theatre; to expand the chronological, geographical, and thematic span of what is considered tragic; as well as to appreciate that tragedy remains a notoriously ill-defined and shifting concept that exists within and alongside a wide array of proximate and overlapping aesthetic ideas. Tragedy may have originally begun with the work of an elite group of men articulating their particular concerns in ancient Athens, and indeed with a specific occasion and specific set of audience expectations, but by the modern period, tragedy had had shaken off many of those foundational constraints and had moved decisively into the realm of those from different class, social, and geographical positions. In future, tragic drama can potentially retain the attention of spectators, students, and scholars by drawing on a range of still more diverse voices, questioning familiar biases, and speaking of those who face renewed disasters and catastrophes in an age of environmental destruction, whilst such drama may continue to foster debate about what exactly the core issues and features that define tragedy might be. As Jennifer Wallace argues, modern tragedy may turn out to be 'uniquely global' in an era when the 'planetary tragedy we are facing now is climate change'. She describes how, 'Caught in an already decided fate and continuing to transgress, we are living in limbo, in a dying planet, as the walking dead'.[8]

Certainly, throughout the twentieth century and into our own age, in a range of disparate and perhaps ever-more demoralizing contexts, new versions of the goat-song have continued to be heard. As Synge put it at the conclusion of *Riders to the Sea*: '*the keen rises a little more loudly from the women, then sinks away*'.[9]

NOTES

Introduction

1   Steiner, *The Death of Tragedy* (London: Faber, 1961), p.316.
2   Steiner, 'Tragedy, Pure and Simple', in *Tragedy and the Tragic*, ed. M.S. Silk (Oxford: Clarendon Press, 1996), p.543.
3   Pavis, *Dictionary of the Theatre*, trans. Christine Shantz (Toronto: University of Toronto Press, 1998), p.414.
4   Winkler and Zeitlin, 'Introduction', in *Nothing to Do with Dionysos?*, ed. John J. Winkler and Froma I. Zeitlin (Princeton: Princeton University Press, 1990), pp.3–11, p.4.
5   Winkler, 'The Ephebes' Song', in *Nothing to Do with Dionysos?*, ed. Winkler and Froma, pp.20–62 (p.37).
6   Hegel, *Hegel's Aesthetics: Lectures on Fine Art*, trans. T.M. Knox, 2 vols (Oxford: Clarendon Press, 1975), p.10.
7   Nietzsche, *The Birth of Tragedy*, trans. Douglas Smith (Oxford: Oxford University Press, 2000), p.63.
8   Lukács, 'The Metaphysics of Tragedy' (1910), in *Soul & Form*, ed. John T. Sanders and Katie Terezakis, trans. Anna Bostock (New York: Columbia University Press, 2010), pp.175–98, p.176.
9   Lukács, 'The Metaphysics of Tragedy', p.176.
10 Lukács, 'The Metaphysics of Tragedy', p.183.
11 Benjamin, *The Origin of German Tragic Drama*, trans. John Osborne (London: Verso, 2003), p.101.
12 Hammond, *Tragicomedy* (London: Bloomsbury, 2021), pp.30–1.
13 Benjamin, *The Origin*, p.112.
14 Camus, 'Lecture Given in Athens on the Future of Tragedy', in *Lyrical and Critical Essays*, ed. and trans. Philip Thody (London: Hamish Hamilton, 1967), pp.177–87, p.177.

15 Camus, 'Lecture Given in Athens on the Future of Tragedy', p.177.

16 Camus, 'Lecture Given in Athens on the Future of Tragedy', p.178, p.180, p.185.

17 Goldmann, *The Hidden God* (London: Routledge, 1964), p.41.

18 Goldmann, *The Hidden God*, p.48.

19 Adorno, 'Cultural Criticism and Society', in *Prisms*, trans. Samuel and Shierry Weber (Cambridge: MIT Press, 1983), pp.17–34, p.34.

20 Adorno, *Aesthetic Theory*, ed. and trans. Robert Hullot-Kentor (London: Bloomsbury, 2013), p.249.

21 Adorno, 'Is Art Lighthearted?', in *Notes to Literature, Volume 2*, trans. Shierry Weber Nicholsen (New York: Columbia University Press, 1992), pp.252–3.

22 McDonald, *Tragedy and Irish Literature* (Houndmills: Palgrave, 2002), p.128.

23 ('La tragédie, pour nous, est un phénomène historique qui triompha entre le XVIe et le XVIIIe siècle'). Sartre, *Un théâtre de situations* (Paris: Gallimard, 1973), p.56. Nonetheless, Sartre had himself adapted the Greek-tragic of Orestes when writing his 1943 play *Les Mouches* ('The Flies').

24 Callaghan, *Woman and Gender in Renaissance Tragedy* (New York and London: Harvester Wheatsheaf, 1989), p.49.

25 Skantze, 'Gender and Sexuality: Watching as Praxis', in Bushnell et al., VI, 145–59 (p.146).

26 Wallace, *Tragedy since 9/11* (London: Bloomsbury, 2020), p.10.

27 Donald Trump, Twitter message of 14 July 2016: Trump was responding to a terrorist attack in Nice, where eighty-four people died.

28 Richards, *Principles of Literary Criticism* (London and New York: Routledge, 2001), p.63.

29 Stefan Collini, 'The "Tragedy" Paper at Cambridge', *Cambridge Authors* <https://www.english.cam.ac.uk/cambridgeauthors/the-tragedy-paper-continuity-and-change/>.

30 Eagleton, *Tragedy* (New Haven: Yale University Press, 2020), p.138.

31 Lehmann, *Tragedy and Dramatic Theatre*, trans. Erik Butler
    (London: Routledge, 2016), p.23.

32 Wilson, 'Introduction', in *A Cultural History of Tragedy*, ed.
    Rebecca Bushnell et al., 6 vols (London: Bloomsbury, 2020), I,
    1–16 (p.7).

33 Plato, *Republic: Books 6–10*, ed. Chris Emlyn-Jones and
    William Preddy (Cambridge, MA: Harvard University Press,
    2013), p.419.

34 Aristotle, *Poetics*, trans. Anthony Kenny (Oxford: Oxford
    University Press, 2013), pp.25–6.

35 Aristotle, *Poetics,* p.54.

36 See Watson, *The Lost Second Book of Aristotle's Poetics*
    (Chicago: University of Chicago Press, 2012).

37 Cooper, *The Tragedy of Philosophy* (Albany: State University of
    New York Press, 2016), p.10.

38 Johnson, 'Modern Philosophy and Greek Tragedy', in *The
    Encyclopedia of Greek Tragedy*, ed. Hanna M. Roisman, 3 vols
    (London: Wiley-Blackwell, 2014), II, 853–59, p.855.

39 Hegel, *Hegel's Aesthetics,* II, 1199.

40 Hegel, *Hegel's Aesthetics,* I, 464.

41 Hegel, *Hegel's Aesthetics,* II, 1158, 1219.

42 Schopenhauer, *The World as Will and Representation*, 2 vols,
    ed. and trans. Judith Norman et al. (Cambridge: Cambridge
    University Press, 2010–18), I, 280.

43 Williams, 'Melodrama', in *The Cambridge History of Victorian
    Literature*, ed. K. Flint (Cambridge: Cambridge University Press,
    2012), pp.193–219, p.195.

44 'The Company at the Prince's Theatre', *Manchester Guardian*,
    7 August 1866, p.5.

45 Shaw, 'Preface: *The Shewing-up of Blanco Posnet*', in *Playlets*,
    ed. James Moran (Oxford: Oxford University Press, 2021),
    pp.217–73, pp.247–8.

46 The notion that Euripides had such doubts is found in the
    comedy of Aristophanes (*c.*450 BCE–388 BCE). In Aristophanes's
    Thesmophoriazusae, one character claims that Euripides' work
    on tragedies 'has got all the men believing that there aren't any

gods', and in the *Frogs* Euripides is described as 'god-detested scum'. *Thesmophoriazusae*, trans. Alan H. Sommerstein (Warminster: Aris & Phillips, 1994), p.61; *Frogs*, trans. Alan H. Sommerstein (Warminster: Aris & Phillips, 1996), p.111.

47   Shaw, 'Preface: *The Shewing-up of Blanco Posnet*', p.261.

48   Walton, 'Hit or Myth', in *Amid Our Troubles*, ed. Marianne McDonald and J. Michael Walton (London: Methuen, 2002), pp.3–36, pp.4–5.

49   Innes, *Edward Gordon Craig* (Amsterdam: Harwood, 1998), p.120.

50   Hall, *Greek Tragedy* (Oxford: Oxford University Press, 2010), p.268.

51   Salter, *Essays on Two Moderns* (London: Sidgwick & Jackson, 1911), p.9.

52   Shaw, *The Drama Observed: Volume III, 1897–1911*, ed. Bernard F. Dukore (University Park, PA: Pennsylvania State University Press, 1993), p.1150.

53   Fischer-Lichte, *Dionysus Resurrection* (Chichester: Wiley-Blackwell, 2014), p.51.

54   Freud, *The Standard Edition of the Complete Psychological Works of Sigmund Freud: Volume IV*, trans. James Strachy (London: Vintage, 2001), p.262.

55   Freud, *The Standard Edition of the Complete Psychological Works of Sigmund Freud,* p.262.

56   Freud, *The Standard Edition of the Complete Psychological Works of Sigmund Freud,* p.265.

57   Shaw, *The Quintessence of Ibsenism*, in Shaw, *Major Critical Essays* (London: Constable, 1932), pp.1–150, p.60.

58   Aristotle, *Poetics,* p.32. Bradley, *Shakespearean Tragedy*, 2nd edn (London: Macmillan, 1919), p.11.

59   Bradley, *Shakespearean Tragedy*, p.8.

60   'Death of a Salesman', *New York Times*, 20 February 1949, p.X1.

61   'S.N., 'Miller Rediscovers Secret of Tragedy', *Washington Post*, 17 June 1949, p.B6; 'Phoenix Theatre', *Times*, 29 July 1949, p.9.

62 Miller, 'Tragedy and the Common Man', *New York Times*, 27 February 1949, p.X1.

63 Williams, *Modern Tragedy* (London: Chatto and Windus, 1966), p.14.

64 Williams, *Modern Tragedy,* p.13.

65 Admittedly, Miller and Williams have some precursors here: George Lillo's *The London Merchant* (1731) anticipates some of this idea of bourgeois tragedy, whilst Nicholas Rowe's 'she-tragedies' of the early eighteenth century move partly towards a bourgeois sphere by focusing on the plight of women.

66 Benjamin, 'What Is Epic Theatre? (II)', in Benjamin, *Selected Writings*, 4 vols, trans. Edmund Jephcott and Others, ed. Howard Eiland and Michael W. Jennings (Cambridge: Harvard University Press, 2003), IV, 302–12, p.304.

67 Brecht, *Collected Plays*, ed. John Willett et al., 8 vols (London: Bloomsbury, 2004), V, 271.

68 Thomson, *Brecht: Mother Courage and Her Children* (Cambridge: Cambridge University Press, 1997), p.119.

69 Szondi, *Theory of the Modern Drama*, ed. and trans. Michael Hays (Cambridge: Polity, 1987 [1956]), p.32.

70 Szondi, *Theory of the Modern Drama*, p.35. Szondi's wider thinking about tragedy was deeply informed by his engagement with Schelling: see Szondi, *An Essay on the Tragic*, trans. Paul Fleming (Stanford: Stanford University Press, 2002), p.9.

71 McGuinness, *Maurice Maeterlinck and the Making of Modern Theatre* (Oxford: Oxford University Press, 2000), p.214.

72 Maeterlinck, *The Treasure of the Humble*, trans. Alfred Sutro (New York: Dodd, Mead & Company, 1912), p.97.

73 Lehmann, *Tragedy and Dramatic Theatre,* p.373.

74 Lehmann, *Tragedy and Dramatic Theatre,* p.10.

75 Goulimari, *Literary Criticism and Theory* (Oxford: Routledge, 2015), p.45.

76 Quayson, *Tragedy and Postcolonial Literature* (Cambridge: Cambridge University Press, 2021), pp.36–8.

77 Scott, 'The Tragic Vision in Postcolonial Time', *PMLA*, 129:4 (2014), 799–808, p.801.

78 Meeker, *The Comedy of Survival: Studies in Literary Ecology* (New York: Scribner, 1974), p.42.

79 Sophocles, *Antigone*, Grene and Lattimore, eds, *The Complete Greek Tragedies: Volume II, Sophocles* (Chicago: University of Chicago Press, 1992), p.174.

80 Meeker, *The Comedy of Survival,* pp.44–5.

81 Estok, 'Doing Ecocriticism with Shakespeare', in *Early Modern Ecostudies*, ed. Thomas Hallock et al. (Houndmills: Palgrave Macmillan, 2008), pp.77–91, p.78.

82 Yeats, 'Certain Noble Plays of Japan', in Yeats, *Collected Works*, ed. Richard J. Finneran et al., 14 vols (New York: Scribner, 1990–2008), IV, 163–73 (p.165).

83 Yeats, *At the Hawk's Well*, in Yeats, II, 297–306 (p.304).

84 Yeats, *At the Hawk's Well*, II, 302.

85 Yeats, *At the Hawk's Well,* II, 303–4.

86 Schmitt, 'Intimations of Immortality: W.B. Yeats's "At the Hawk's Well"', *Theatre Journal*, 31:4 (1979), 501–10, pp.503–4.

87 Wilson, 'Introduction', in Bushnell et al., p.3.

88 Casey, 'An Aran Requiem', in *Critical Essays on John Millington Synge*, ed. Daniel J. Casey (New York: G.K. Hall, 1994), pp.88–97, p.91.

89 Kennedy, 'Sympathy between Man and Nature', *Interdisciplinary Studies in Literature and Environment*, 11:1 (2004), 15–30 (p.15). Eagleton, *Sweet Violence: A Study of the Tragic* (Oxford: Blackwell, 2002), p.128.

Chapter 1

1 Roberts, 'The Plays of Synge', *Irish Times*, 2 August 1955, p.5.

2 'Irish National Theatre', *Irish Daily Independent and Nation*, 26 February 1904, p.5.

3 [Arthur Griffith], 'All Ireland', *United Irishman*, 5 March 1904, p.1.

4 'Irish National Theatre Society', *Irish Times*, 26 February 1904, p.5.

5 Hill, *Our Dramatic Heritage: Volume 5*, ed. Philip G. Hill (Rutherford: Fairleigh Dickinson University Press, 1991), p.175.

6 Welch, *The Abbey Theatre, 1899–1999* (Oxford: Oxford University Press, 1999), p.39.

7 Lecossois, *Performance, Modernity and the Plays of J.M. Synge* (Cambridge: Cambridge University Press, 2021), p.164, p.35.

8 Marlowe, *Doctor Faustus, A-Text*, in *Doctor Faustus and Other Plays*, ed. David Bevington and Eric Rasmussen (Oxford: Oxford University Press, 1995), pp.137–83, p.183. The line was written by John Butler Yeats in his diary when he learnt of Synge's death: see J.B. Yeats, MS. Holo. 850. & TS signed. 'John Synge is Dead'. New York Public Library, Astor, Lenox and Tilden Foundations Rare Books and Manuscripts Division. Foster-Murphy Collection, box 14, f.3.

9 Synge, *Riders to the Sea*, Synge, *Collected Works*, 4 vols, ed. Robin Skelton et al. (London: Oxford University Press, 1962–8), III, 1–27, pp.23–7.

10 Yeats, 'Plain Man's *Oedipus*', in Yeats, *Collected Works*, X, 244–5.

11 Gogarty, *As I Was Going Down Sackville Street* (London: Rich & Cowan, 1937), p.289.

12 Trinity College Dublin, MS 4413 f.24r; and Trinity College Dublin, MS 4412, f.27v. I am grateful to Chris Collins for his help in locating these sources.

13 Trinity College Dublin, MS 4413 f.24r and Trinity College Dublin, MS 4412, f.27v.

14 Church, *Stories from the Greek Tragedians* (London: Seeley, Jackson & Halliday, 1880), p.148, p.229.

15 Church, *Stories from the Greek Tragedians,* p.95.

16 Church, *Stories from the Greek Tragedians,* p.82.

17 Synge, *Collected Works*, III, 21–7.

18 Holloway, *Joseph Holloway's Abbey Theatre*, ed. Robert Hogan and Michael J. O'Neill (Carbondale: Southern Illinois University Press, 1967), p.35.

19 'Irish Plays in London', *Manchester Guardian*, 28 March 1904, p.4.

20 'Irish Players in Sad Play', *New York Times*, 5 December 1911, p.9.

21 See, for instance, Boyd, *Ireland's Literary Renaissance* (New York: Barnes & Noble, 1916), p.322; or Lloyd, 'Playboy of the Ancient World?', *Classics Ireland*, 18 (2011), 52–68, p.54.

22 Hölderlin, *The Death of Empedocles*, trans. David Farrell Krell (Albany: State University of New York Press, 2008), p.126.

23 Steiner, '"Tragedy" Reconsidered', *New Literary History*, 35:1 (2004), 1–15 (10).

24 Steiner, '"Tragedy" Reconsidered', p.10.

25 Synge, *Collected Works*, III, 23.

26 Steiner, '"Tragedy" Reconsidered', p.11.

27 McCrea, 'Style and Idiom', in *The Cambridge Companion to Irish Modernism*, ed. Joe Cleary (Cambridge: Cambridge University Press, 2014), pp.35–50, p.67.

28 Synge, 'Preface', in *Collected Works*, IV, 53–4, p.53.

29 Synge, *Collected Works*, III, 15.

30 Kiberd, 'J.M. Synge: "A Faker of Peasant Speech"?', *Review of English Studies*, 30:117 (1979), 59–63, p.59.

31 Synge, *Collected Works*, III, 9.

32 See Robinson, *Stones of Aran: Pilgrimage* (London: Penguin, 1990), pp.148–52.

33 See Bourgeois, *John Millington Synge and the Irish Theatre* (London: Constable, 1913), p.139. For later criticism that contradicts Bourgeois, see Skelton, 'The Politics of J.M. Synge', *The Massachusetts Review*, 18:1 (1977), 7–22 and Hewitt, *J.M. Synge: Nature, Politics, Modernism* (Oxford: Oxford University Press, 2021).

34 McCrea, 'Style and Idiom', p.67.

35 Steiner, '"Tragedy" Reconsidered', p.11.

36 Synge, *Collected Works*, III, 27.

37 See Gerstenberger, *John Millington Synge* (New York: Twayne, 1965), p.46 and Cardullo, '"Riders to the Sea": A New View', *Canadian Journal of Irish Studies*, 10:1 (1984), 95–112 (p.95, p.101).

38 Sophocles, *Sophocles: Plays, Oedipus Coloneus*, trans. R.C. Jebb (London: Bristol Classical Press, 2004), p.272.

39 Sophocles, *Oedipus the King, Oedipus at Colonus, Antigone*, trans. F. Storr (London: Heinemann, 1912), pp.307.

40 For instance, Yeats's version of *Oedipus at Colonus* (1934) has a final line that echoes Synge's fatalism and reference to the deity. See Yeats, *Plays*, p.441. More recently, in 2005, Eamon Grennan and Rachel Kitzinger included in the final lines of *Oedipus at Colonus*: 'But cease now, cease your keening' (Sophocles, *Oedipus at Colonus*, trans. Eamon Grennan and Rachel Kitzinger (Oxford: Oxford University Press, 2005), p.104).

41 Synge manuscripts, Trinity College Dublin, letter 109, translated by Kiberd in 'J.M. Synge', p.61.

42 Kiberd, 'J.M. Synge', p.63.

43 Miller, 'Tragedy and the Common Man', p.X1.

44 Synge, *Collected Works*, III, 5, 9.

45 Masefield, *John M. Synge: A Few Personal Recollections, with Biographical Notes* (Dundrum: Cuala Press, 1915), p.14.

46 Masefield, 'Author's Note', in *The Tragedy of Nan* (New York: Macmillan, 1921), pp.vii–viii, p.vii.

47 Masefield, 'Author's Note', p.viii.

48 Masefield, *The Tragedy of Nan, and Other Plays* (New York: Macmillan, 1921), p.15.

49 Lawrence, *The Letters of D.H. Lawrence*, ed. James Boulton et al., 8 vols (Cambridge: Cambridge University Press, 1979–2001), I, 260–1.

50 Lawrence, *The Widowing of Mrs Holroyd*, in Lawrence, *The Plays*, ed. Hans-Wilhelm Schwarze and John Worthen, 2 vols (Cambridge: Cambridge University Press, 2002), I, 61–110 (p.72).

51 'At the Pit-Head', *Manchester Guardian*, 14 December 1926, p.15.

52 Eagleton, *Sweet Violence*, p.183. Lawrence, *Plays*, I, 63.

53 Lawrence, 'Preface to *Touch and Go*', in Lawrence, *Plays*, II, 363–8, pp.365–6.

54 Maeterlinck, *The Treasure of the Humble*, p.103.

55 Maeterlinck, *The Treasure of the Humble*, p.97.

56 Maeterlinck, *The Treasure of the Humble*, p.101, 104.

57 Materlinck, *The Treasure of the Humble*, p.102.

58 Gorman, *James Joyce: A Definitive Biography* (London: Bodley Head, 1941), p.101.

59 Joyce, *Letters of James Joyce*, ed. Stuart Gilbert and Richard Ellmann, 3 vols (London: Faber, 1957–66), II, 35.

60 Quoted by Ellmann, *James Joyce*, rev. edn (Oxford: Oxford University Press, 1982), p.123.

61 Joyce, *A Portrait of the Artist as a Young Man*, ed. Jeri Johnson (Oxford: Oxford University Press, 2000), p.172.

62 Joyce, *My Brother's Keeper*, ed. Richard Ellmann (London: Faber, 1957), p.214.

63 Harry Ransom Center, Joyce collection, box 1 folder 7, J.M. Synge *Riders to the Sea* (1905) translated into Italian by James Joyce and Nicolo Vidacovich, nd, 26pp, fols 4–6. For more on this see James Moran, *Modernists and the Theatre* (London: Bloomsbury, 2022), pp.103–4.

64 Fogarty, 'Ghostly Intertexts', in *Synge and Edwardian Ireland*, ed. Brian Cliff and Nicholas Grene (Cambridge: Cambridge University Press, 2012), pp.225–43, p.231, p.229.

65 Synge, *Collected Works*, III, 30.

66 Fordham, *Lots of Fun at Finnegans Wake* (Oxford: Oxford University Press, 2007), p.15.

67 Kitcher, *Joyce's Kaleidoscope* (Oxford: Oxford University Press, 2007), p.6.

68 Joyce, *Finnegans Wake* (London: Penguin, 1992), p.628. Synge, *Collected Works*, III, 9.

69 See Gifford, *British Film Catalogue: Volume 1*, 3rd edn (London: Routledge, 2001), p.431. Rabaud, *L'appel de la mer* (Paris: Max Eschig, 1924). Mirchandani, *Marga Richter* (Urbana: University of Illinois Press, 2012), p.100. Bruchhäuser, *Komponisten der Gegenwart im Deutschen Komponisten-Interessenverband: ein Handbuch* (Berlin: Deutscher Komponisten-Interessenverband, 1995), p.987. Vaughan Williams, *Riders to the Sea* (London: Oxford University Press, 1936).

70 Lehmann, *Tragedy and Dramatic Theatre*, p.10.

71 Cardullo, '"Riders to the Sea": A New View', p.104.

72 Cardullo, '"Riders to the Sea": A New View', p.104.

73 Joyce, *Finnegans Wake*, p.628.

74 Synge, *Collected Works*, II, p.75.

75 Synge, *Collected Works*, II, p.75.

76 McDonald, *Tragedy and Irish Literature,* p.56.

77 McDonald, *Tragedy and Irish Literature,* p.57.

78 Synge, *Collected Works*, III, 25.

79 Synge, *Collected Works*, III, 23–5.

80 Kennedy, 'Sympathy between Man and Nature', p.21.

81 Synge, *Collected Works*, II, 128, 110.

82 Synge read Nietzsche's *Thus Spoke Zarathustra* on Sunday
    4 April 1897 in Paris (Trinity College Dublin, MS 4418, 25v).
    It is possible that Synge also read *The Birth of Tragedy*. Synge's
    biographer, William McCormack, writes, 'It seems unlikely that
    the author of *Riders to the Sea*, having read *Zarathustra*, omitted
    to read the shorter, more focussed work'. McCormack, *Fool of
    the Family* (London: Weidenfeld & Nicolson, 2000), p.199.

83 Nietzsche, *The Birth of Tragedy*, pp.22–3.

84 Hallman, 'Nietzsche's Environmental Ethics', *Environmental
    Ethics*, 13 (1991), 99–125 and Garrad, *Ecocriticism*, 2nd edn
    (London: Routledge, 2012), p.98.

85 White and Hellerich, 'The Ecological Self: Humanity and
    Nature in Nietzsche and Goethe', *The European Legacy*, 3:3
    (1998), 39–61, p.31.

86 Nietzsche, 'Homer's Contest', in '*On the Genealogy of Morality'
    and Other Writings*, ed. Keith Ansell-Pearson, trans. Carol
    Diethe (Cambridge: Cambridge University Press, 2007),
    pp.174–81, p.174.

87 Drenthen, 'Wildness as a Critical Border Concept',
    Environmental Values, 14 (2005), 317–37 (p.322).

88 Lavrin, *Nietzsche: An Approach* (London: Routledge, 2010
    [1948]), p.22.

89 Nietzsche, *The Birth of Tragedy*, p.60.

90 Hammond, *The Strangeness of Tragedy* (Oxford: Oxford
    University Press, 2009), p.37.

91   Nietzsche, *The Birth of Tragedy*, p.22.

92   Robinson, Bohannan, and Young, 'From Structure to Function', *Microbiology and Molecular Biology Reviews*, 74:3 (2010), 453–76, p.453.

93   Synge, *Collected Works*, II, 9–10.

94   Hewitt, *J.M. Synge*, p.57.

95   Hewitt, *J.M. Synge*, p.68.

96   Aristotle, *Poetics*, p.32. Bradley, *Shakespearean Tragedy*, p.11.

97   Synge, *Collected Works*, III, 17.

98   Hewitt, *J.M. Synge*, p.101.

99   Synge, *Collected Works*, II, 59.

100   Synge, *Collected Works*, II, 58–9.

101   Synge, *Collected Works*, II, 58.

102   See Nietzsche '*On the Genealogy of Morality' and Other Writings*, p.37.

103   Acampora, 'Using and Abusing Nietzsche for Environmental Ethics', *Environmental Ethics*, 16 (1994), 187–94.

104   Yeats, 'The Tragic Theatre', in Yeats, IV, 174–9 (p.174).

105   Yeats, 'The Tragic Theatre', IV, 177.

106   Bohlmann, *Yeats and Nietzsche* (London: Macmillan, 1982), p.62.

107   Yeats, 'The Tragic Theatre', IV, 176–8.

108   For more on the tragic dimensions of Yeats's *Four Plays for Dancers*, see Lehmann, *Tragedy and Dramatic Theatre*, pp.381–2, and Good, *W.B. Yeats and the Creation of a Tragic Universe* (London: Macmillan, 1987), p.34.

109   Morash, *Yeats on Theatre* (Cambridge: Cambridge University Press, 2021), p.106.

110   Yeats, 'The Tragic Theatre', II, 301, 306.

111   Yeats, 'The Tragic Theatre', II, 304.

112   Ellis, *The Plays of W.B. Yeats* (Basingstoke: Macmillan, 1995), p.226.

113   Yeats, 'The Tragic Theatre', II, 297–9.

114   Schmitt, 'Intimations of Immortality', p.503.

115   Yeats, 'The Tragic Theatre', II, 298.

116 Yeats, 'The Tragic Theatre', II, 313, 308.

117 Yeats, 'The Tragic Theatre', II, 319.

118 Yeats, 'The Tragic Theatre', II, 310.

119 Yeats, 'The Tragic Theatre', II, 315.

120 Yeats, 'The Tragic Theatre', II, 455.

121 Yeats, 'The Tragic Theatre', II, 706.

122 Meeker, *The Comedy of Survival,* p.44.

123 Heise, *Sense of Place and Sense of Planet* (Oxford: Oxford University Press, 2008), p.5.

124 Steiner, '"Tragedy", Reconsidered', p.31.

125 Harari, *Sapiens: A Brief History of Humankind* (London: Harvill Secker, 2014), pp.73–4.

126 Milne, 'Sites of Performance and Circulation', in Bushnell et al., VI, 41–56 (p.48).

Chapter 2

1 Enrique Moradiellos, *Franco* ([?]: I.B. Tauris: 2017), p.101.

2 Hayman, *Brecht* (London: Weidenfeld and Nicolson, 1983), p.200.

3 Parker, *Bertolt Brecht* (London: Bloomsbury, 2014), p.366.

4 Kuhn and Willett, 'Introduction', Brecht, *Collected Plays*, IV, vii–xxix (p.xvi).

5 Jacobs and Ohlsen, eds, *Bertolt Brecht in Britain* (London: TQ Publications, 1976), p.29.

6 Of course, some people in Britain already knew a version of Brecht's name: *The Times* reviewed the German production of *The Threepenny Opera* in September 1928, where he was named as 'Kurt Brecht' ('The Threepenny Opera', *The Times*, 25 September 1928, p.12). By 1939, when *Señora Carrar's Rifles* reached Scotland the piece was advertised and reviewed as an 'acclaimed' drama 'by Berthola Brecht' ('A.R.P. in Falkirk', *Falkirk Herald*, 18 January 1939, p.2. 'Falkirk Peace Council', *Falkirk Herald*, 14 January 1939, p.1).

7   Susan Cannon Harris, 'Mobilizing Maurya', *Modern Drama*, 56:1 (2013), 38–59, p.40.

8   Synge, *Collected Works*, III, 23.

9   Brecht, *Señora Carrar's Rifles*, in Brecht, *Collected Plays*, IV, 207–36 (p.234).

10   Esslin, *Brecht* (London: Eyre Methuen, 1963), p.270, p.60.

11   Roche, 'Synge, Brecht, and the Hiberno-German Connection', *Hungarian Journal of English and American Studies*, 10:1/2 (2004), 9–32.

12   Dickson, *Towards Utopia* (Oxford: Clarendon, 1978), p.107.

13   Cannon Harris, 'Mobilizing Maurya', pp.43–4.

14   Marx, *Grundrisse*, trans. Martin Nicolaus (London: Vintage, 1973), p.110.

15   Hegel, *Hegel's Aesthetics*, p.480.

16   Korsch, *Kernpunkte der materialistischen Geschichtsauffassung* (Leipzig: C.L. Hirschfeld, 1922), p.54. Brecht scholars have debated the influence of Korsch upon Brecht ever since Wolfdietrich Rasch's 'Bertolt Brechts marxistischer Lehrer', *Zur deutschen Literatur seit der Jahrhundertwende, Gesammelte Aufsätze* (Stuttgart: Metzler, 1967), pp.243–73.

17   Brecht, 'Key Points in Korsch, pp.37 and 54', in *Brecht on Art and Politics*, ed. and trans. Thomas Kuhn and Steve Giles (London: Methuen, 2003), pp.109–10.

18   Brecht, 'Key Points in Korsch', p.109.

19   Brecht, 'Key Points in Korsch', pp.109–10.

20   Synge, *Collected Works*, III, 27.

21   Brecht, 'Theatre for Pleasure or Theatre for Instruction', in *Brecht on Theatre*, ed. Steve Giles et al., rev. 3rd edn (London: Bloomsbury, 2015), pp.109–17, p.112.

22   Brecht, 'Short Organon for the Theatre', in *Brecht on Theatre*, pp.229–63, p.239.

23   Brecht, 'Key Points in Korsch', p.110.

24   Gray, 'Brecht and Tragedy', *Cambridge Quarterly*, 8:3 (1979), 236–49 (p.242).

25   Brecht, 'Key Points in Korsch', p.110.

26 Brecht, 'Miscellaneous Texts', in *Brecht on Performance*, ed. Steve Giles et al. (London: Bloomsbury, 2018), pp.97–118, p.98.

27 Brecht, *Collected Plays*, IV, 235–6.

28 Brecht, 'The German Drama: Pre-Hitler', in *Brecht on Theatre*, pp.119–24, p.122.

29 'Plays of the Week', *The Era*, 15 September 1938, p.11.

30 'Plays and Pictures', *New Statesman and Nation*, 17 September 1938, p.417.

31 Quoted by Esslin p.60.

32 'Plays at Wylam', *Newcastle Evening Chronicle*, 31 March 1939, p.5.

33 'A.R.P. in Falkirk', *Falkirk Herald*, 18 January 1939, p.2.

34 'Appeal for Food', *Scotsman*, 21 November 1938, p.10.

35 Brecht, *Brecht on Theatre*, p.112.

36 Brecht, 'Dialogue on Acting', in *Brecht on Theatre*, pp.45–8, pp.47–8.

37 Quoted by Ewen, *Bertolt Brecht* (London: Calder & Boyars, 1970), p.318.

38 Brecht, 'Dialogue about an Actress of the Epic Theatre', in Brecht, *Collected Plays*, IV, 358–60 (p.359).

39 Brecht, 'Prologue to "Señora Carrar's Rifles"', in Brecht, *Collected Plays*, IV, 360–1 (p.360).

40 Brecht, *Collected Plays*, IV, 359.

41 Brecht, 'Epilogue to "Señora Carrar's Rifles"', in Brecht, *Collected Plays*, IV, 362.

42 Brecht, *Messingkauf, or Buying Brass*, in *Brecht on Performance*, pp.1–141, p.35.

43 Brecht, *Brecht on Performance*, p.35.

44 Brecht, *Brecht on Performance*, p.57.

45 Steiner, *The Death of Tragedy*, p.274. Brecht, 'Productive Obstacles', in *Brecht on Theatre*, p.251.

46 Nelson, 'The Birth of Tragedy out of Pedagogy', *The German Quarterly*, 46:4 (1973), 566–80 (p.566).

47 Goldhill, *Sophocles and the Language of Tragedy* (Oxford: Oxford University Press, 2012), p.54.

48 Brecht, 'On *The Antigone of Sophocles* (1947–8) from *Antigone Model 1948*', in Brecht, *Brecht on Performance*, pp.163–80, p.166.

49 See Cohn, *Modern Shakespeare Offshoots* (Princeton: Princeton University Press, 1976), p.341.

50 Brecht, *The Antigone of Sophocles*, in Brecht, *Brecht: Collected Plays,* VIII, 1–51 (pp.5–6).

51 Brecht, *Collected Plays*, VIII, 7.

52 Benjamin, 'What Is Epic Theatre? (II)', p.303.

53 Brecht, *Stücke: XI* (Frankfurt am Main: Suhrkamp Verlag, 1959), p.29, p.31.

54 Brecht, *Stücke: XI*, pp.87–8, see also p.89 and p.92. Translation here from Brecht, *Collected Plays*, VIII, 46.

55 Brecht, *Collected Plays*, VIII, 18.

56 Brecht, *Collected Plays*, VIII, 25.

57 Brecht, *Collected Plays*, VIII, 44.

58 Tom Kuhn and David Constantine, 'Editorial Notes', in Brecht, *Collected Plays*, VIII, 219–22 (p.220). For the production at Greiz in 1951, Brecht removed the prelude set in Berlin in 1945, and instead replaced it with a new prologue: a speech (by Tiresias) telling the audience: 'We ask you/ To look into your own hearts and minds for similar deeds' (Brecht, 'New Prologue to "Antigone", 1951', in Brecht, *Collected Plays*, VIII, 218).

59 Beckett, *Proust and Three Dialogues with Georges Duthuit* (London: John Calder, 1965), p.67.

60 Schopenhauer, *The World*, I, 279–80.

61 Schopenhauer, *The World*, I, 281.

62 Schopenhauer, *The World*, I, 281.

63 Pilling, 'Beckett's *Proust*', *Journal of Beckett Studies*, I (1976), 8–29, p.12.

64 Yeats, *Plays*, p.432. Spence, 'Sophoclean Beckett in Performance', *Skenè: Journal of Theatre and Drama Studies*, 2:2 (2016), 177–201 (p.178).

65 Beckett, *Waiting for Godot*, 2nd edn (London: Faber, 1965), p.11.

66 Steiner, *Grammars of Creation* (New Haven: Yale University Press, 2002), p.254. Spence, p.178.

67 Beckett, 'Notebook with dark red covers, inscribed on the front cover in capitals "WHOROSCOPE", 11 x 17cm, Undated', University of Reading, BC MS 3000/1, f.74r, (c) the Estate of Samuel Beckett.

68 Beckett, 'Notebook', f.74r, (c) the Estate of Samuel Beckett.

69 Beckett, 'Notebook', f.74r, (c) the Estate of Samuel Beckett.

70 Beckett, 'Notebook', f.75, (c) the Estate of Samuel Beckett.

71 Schopenhauer, *The World*, I, 281–2.

72 Schopenhauer, *The World*, I, 282.

73 Hegel, *Hegel's Aesthetics,* II, 1178.

74 Erickson, 'Is Nothing to Be Done?', *Modern Drama*, 50:2 (2007), 258–75 (p.259).

75 Newton, *Modern Literature and the Tragic* (Edinburgh: Edinburgh University Press, 2008), p.145.

76 Kruse, 'Tragicomedy and Tragic Burlesque', *Sydney Studies in English*, 1 (1975), 76–96 (p.81).

77 Knowlson, *Damned to Fame* (New York: Simon & Schuster, 1996), p.71.

78 Erickson, 'Is Nothing to Be Done?', p.269.

79 Schopenhauer, 'Supplement I: An Essay on Visions and Matters Connected Therewith', Wagner, *Beethoven: With a Supplement from the Philosophical Works of Arthur Schopenhauer*, trans. Edward Dannreuther (London: W.M. Reeves, 1903), pp.115–53, p.153. See TCD MS 4414, f.49v.

80 Marx, *Grundrisse*, p.110.

81 Beckett, *Waiting for Godot,* p.9.

82 Beckett, *Waiting for Godot*, p.54, p.94.

83 Schopenhauer, *The World*, II, 454.

84 Brecht, *Collected Plays*, IV, 235–6.

85 Williams, 'Theatre as a Political Forum', in *Visions and Blueprints*, ed. Edward Timms and Peter Collier (Manchester: Manchester University Press, 1988), pp.307–20, p.320.

86 Curtis, *Bitter Lake*, Prod. Lucy Kelsall, BBC, 25 January 2015.

87 Surkov, *Almost Zero*, trans. Nino Gojiashvili and Nastya Valentine, Kindle Edition, location 37 of 3094.

88 Quoted by Pomerantsev, *Nothing Is True and Everything Is Possible* (London: Faber, 2015), p.82.

89 Hughes, 'Boris Johnson Accuses Labour of "outrageous politicking" over Grenfell Tower Tragedy', *Telegraph*, 16 June 2017 <https://www.telegraph.co.uk/news/2017/06/16/boris-johnson-accuses-labour-outrageous-politicking-grenfell/>.

90 'Mitt Romney's Speech on the Shotting in Colorado', *Real Clear Politics*, 20 July 2012, https://www.realclearpolitics.com/articles/2012/07/20/mitt_romneys_speech_on_the_shooting_in_colorado_114876.html.

91 Hill, 'Stop Calling Breonna Taylor's Killing a "Tragedy"', *The Atlantic*, <https://www.theatlantic.com/ideas/archive/2020/09/tragedy-means-blaming-black-people/616528/>.

92 See Ionica, *The Affects, Cognition and Politics of Samuel Beckett's Postwar Drama* (Cham: Palgrave Macmillan, 2020), p.16.

93 Jameson, *Brecht and Method* (London: Verso, 1998), p.14.

94 Nadel, 'Beckett's Holocaust', in *The Palgrave Handbook of Holocaust Literature and Culture*, ed. Victoria Aarons and Phyllis Lassner (Cham: Palgrave Macmillan, 2020), pp.697–705, p.689.

95 Morin, *Beckett's Political Imagination* (Cambridge: Cambridge University Press, 2017), p.1.

96 Die Archivbibliothek des Bertolt Brecht, Akademie der Küste, 1061/4, quoted by Werner Hecht, 'Brecht "und" Beckett', *Theater der Zeit*, 21:14 (August 1966), 28–30 (p.28).

97 In the Suhrkamp edition, the deletions read as follows:
    Estragon: Ich erinnere mich an die Karten vom heiligen Land. Bunte Karten.
    Das Tote Meer war blassblau. Wenn ich nur hinguckte, hatte ich schon Durst.
    The reversed lines then read:
    Estragon: Ich hör zu. Du hättest Dichter werden sollen.
    Wladimir: War ich doch. (Er zeigt auf seine Lumpen) Sieht man das nicht.
    Die Archivbibliothek des Bertolt Brecht, Akademie der Küste, 1061/6, quoted by Werner Hecht, p.29.

98 Die Archivbibliothek des Bertolt Brecht, Akademie der Küste, 1061/10, quoted by Werner Hecht, p.29.

99 Brecht, 'Stage Design in the Epic Theatre', in *Brecht on Theatre*, p.189.

100 Rülicke-Weiler, *Die Dramaturgie Brechts* (Berlin: Henschelverlag Kunst und Gesellschaft, 1968), pp.154–6.

101 Brecht, *Brecht on Performance*, p.171.

102 Brecht, 'Kurt Palm', in *Brecht on Theatre*, pp.272–4, p.273.

103 Benjamin, 'What Is Epic Theatre? [I]', Benjamin, *Understanding Brecht*, trans. Anna Bostock (London: Verso, 2003), pp.1–15, p.1.

Chapter 3

1 Jaspers, *Tragedy Is Not Enough*, trans. H. A. T. Reiche et al. (London: Victor Gollancz, 1953), p.31, p.33.

2 Taplin, *Greek Fire* (New York: Atheneum, 1990), pp.4–5.

3 Taplin, *Greek Fire,* p.4, p.ii.

4 Wetmore, *Black Dionysus* (Jefferson: McFarland, 2003), p.3.

5 Reiss, *Against Autonomy* (Stanford: Stanford University Press, 2002), p.145.

6 Scott, 'The Tragic Vision in Postcolonial Time', p.800.

7 Harmsen, Ellis, and Devaux, *A History of St Lucia* (Vieux Fort: Lighthouse Road, 2012), p.91, p.121, p.321.

8 Aboelazm, 'Reworking John Millington Synge's *Riders to the Sea*', *330-2011 2nd International Conference on Humanities, Historical and Social Sciences IPEDR*, 17 (2011), 330–4 (p.331).

9 Thieme, *Derek Walcott* (Manchester: Manchester University Press, 1999), p.42.

10 Quoted by Thieme, *Derek Walcott*, p.42.

11 Thieme, *Derek Walcott*, p.42.

12 'Trinidad and Tobago', in *The Cambridge Guide to African and Caribbean Theatre*, ed. Martin Banham, Errol Hill and George Woodyard (Cambridge: Cambridge University Press, 1994), pp.225–48, pp.231–2.

13 Walcott's remarks to Edward Hirsch reprinted in Breslin,
    Nobody's Nation (Chicago: University of Chicago Press, 2001),
    pp.86–7.

14 Slade Hopkinson quote in Breslin, *Nobody's Nation,* p.87.
    Walcott published two different versions of the play: in the
    script first published in the *Tamarack Review* in 1960, the
    dialogue revolves around the St Lucian creole. But Walcott soon
    realized that even a wider West Indian audience in places such
    as Jamaica could not easily access that creole, and so when he
    published a revised version of the play ten years later Walcott
    altered much of the dialogue. Phrases from the 1960 version
    such as 'Ki ça?' and 'Ous menti!' became in the 1970s script
    'What' and 'You lie'. Walcott, *The Sea at Dauphin,* in *Tamarack
    Review,* 14 (1960), 76–95, p.83. Walcott, *The Sea at Dauphin,*
    in Walcott, *Dream on Monkey Mountain and Other Plays*
    (New York: Farrar, Straus and Giroux, 1971), pp.41–80, p.58.

15 Harmsen, Ellis, and Devaux, *A History of St Lucia,* p.306.

16 Elsewhere, the Black writer and civil rights activist James
    Weldon Johnson had already identified Synge's usefulness
    for those communities whose language had been denigrated:
    when Johnson wrote the prefaces to his 1922 and 1931 poetry
    anthologies, *God's Trombones: Seven Negro Sermons in Verse,*
    he declared: 'What the colored poet in the United States needs
    to do is something like what Synge did for the Irish; he needs to
    find a form which will express the racial spirit by symbols from
    within'. Johnson, *God's Trombones: Seven Negro Sermons in
    Verse* (London: Penguin, 2008), p.6.

17 Hirsch and Walcott, 'An Interview with Derek Walcott',
    Contemporary Literature, 20:3 (1979), 279–92 (p.288).

18 Hirsch and Walcott, 'An Interview with Derek Walcott',
    p.288.

19 Walcott, *The Sea at Dauphin,* in *Dream on Monkey Mountain,*
    p.80.

20 Synge, *Collected Works,* III, 27.

21 Walcott, *Conversations with Derek Walcott,* ed. William Baer
    (Jackson: University Press of Mississippi, 1996), p.60.

22 Reiss, *Against Autonomy,* p.138.

23 Malouf, 'Dissimilation and Federation: Irish and Caribbean
    Modernisms in Derek Walcott's *The Sea at Dauphin*', in
    Comparative American Studies An International Journal, 8:2
    (2010), 140–54 (p.146).

24 Reiss, *Against Autonomy,* p.506.

25 Reiss, *Against Autonomy,* p.506. *Oedipus Rex*, in Sophocles,
    The Complete Plays, ed. Grene and Lattimore, pp.68–9.

26 Synge, *Collected Works*, III, 11.

27 Synge, *Collected Works*, III, 27.

28 Reiss, *Against Autonomy,* p.506.

29 Quayson, *Tragedy*, p.11.

30 Reiss, *Against Autonomy,* p.506.

31 Synge, *Collected Works*, III, 11.

32 Synge, *Collected Works*, III, 25, 27.

33 Synge, *Collected Works*, III, 27.

34 Walcott, *The Sea at Dauphin*, in Walcott, *Dream on Monkey
    Mountain*, p.47.

35 Walcott, *The Sea at Dauphin*, in Walcott, *Dream on Monkey
    Mountain*, p.68.

36 Walcott, *The Sea at Dauphin*, in Walcott, *Dream on Monkey
    Mountain*, p.61.

37 Nchia, '"As it was in the Beginning …": Religious Fanaticism
    and the Quest for a New Messiah in the Plays of Derek Walcott
    and Bate Besong', in *Re-writing Past, Imagining Futures*, ed.
    Victor N. Gomia and Gilbert S. Ndi (Denver: Spears, 2017),
    pp.56–71, p.60.

38 Walcott, *The Sea at Dauphin*, in Walcott, *Dream on Monkey
    Mountain*, p.61.

39 Synge, *Collected Works*, III, 21.

40 Synge, *Collected Works*, III, 27.

41 Walcott, *The Sea at Dauphin*, in Walcott, *Dream on Monkey
    Mountain*, p.73.

42 Sarkar, 'Existence as Self-making in Derek Walcott's *Sea at
    Dauphin*', *Anthurium*, 14:2 (2018), 1–13 (p.3).

43 Walcott, *Conversations with Derek Walcott*, p.24.

44 Quayson, *Tragedy*, p.14. Kiberd, *Inventing Ireland* (London: Jonathan Cape, 1995), p.45.

45 Breslin, *Nobody's Nation,* p.85.

46 Siga Asanga, 'Theory and Practice in the Plays of John Pepper Clark and Wole Soyinka', University of Ottowa, PhD thesis, 1978, p.1.

47 Nwakanma, *Christopher Okigbo, 1930–67* (Woodbridge: James Currey, 2010), p.80

48 Agarwalla, *The African Poetry and Drama* (New Delhi: Prestige, 2000), p.68. At an early stage, the university's teaching staff also included D.E.S. Maxwell, a scholar of Irish literature who, in 1965, edited a book on W.B. Yeats, and in 1973 published the first major study of Brian Friel. Maxwell also published *A Critical History of Modern Irish Drama*, where he showed himself alive to the politics of theatrical production under colonialism, and later acted as one of the editors of the *Field Day Anthology of Irish Writing*, which has a broad metanarrative about colonialism and resistance (Maxwell, *A Critical History of Modern Irish Drama* (Cambridge: Cambridge University Press, 1984), p.22).

49 Udo, *Geographical Regions of Nigeria* (Oakland: University of California Press, 1970), p.58.

50 Asanga, 'Theory and Practice in the Plays of John Pepper Clark and Wole Soyinka', p.6.

51 Currey, 'Literary Publishing after Nigerian Independence', *Research in African Literatures*, 44:2 (2013), 8–16 (pp.9–10).

52 Clark, *Song of a Goat*, in Clark, *Three Plays* (London and Ibadan: Oxford University Press, 1964), pp.1–48, p.2.

53 Clark, *Song*, p.5.

54 See Falola and Heaton, *A History of Nigeria* (Cambridge: Cambridge University Press, 2008), pp.134–5, p.172.

55 Okagbue, 'Nigeria', in *The Continuum Companion to Twentieth Century Theatre*, ed. Colin Chambers (London: Continuum, 2002), pp.549–51, p.550.

56 King, *From New National to World Literature* (Stuttgart: Ibidem, 2016), p.42.

57 King, *From New National to World Literature*, p.44.

58 Scott, 'The Tragic Vision in Postcolonial Time', p.801.

59 Camus, 'Lecture Given in Athens on the Future of Tragedy', p.177.

60 Camus, 'Lecture Given in Athens on the Future of Tragedy', p.177.

61 Camus, 'Lecture Given in Athens on the Future of Tragedy', p.179.

62 Scott, 'The Tragic Vision in Postcolonial Time', p.801.

63 Soyinka, *Myth, Literature and the African World* (Cambridge: Cambridge University Press, 1976), p.50.

64 Soyinka, *Myth, Literature and the African World*, p.50.

65 Synge, *Collected Works*, III, 21, 23.

66 Clark, *Song*, p.44.

67 Soyinka, *Myth, Literature and the African World*, p.51.

68 Banham, 'Nigerian Dramatists', *Journal of Commonwealth Literature* 7 (1969), 132–6 (pp.132–3).

69 Soyinka, *Myth, Literature and the African World*, p.45.

70 Wetmore, *Black Dionysus,* p.71.

71 Povey, 'West African Drama in English', *Comparative Drama*, 1:2 (1967), 110–21 (p.119).

72 Clark, *Song*, p.42.

73 Clark, *Song*, p.42.

74 Clark, *Song*, p.44.

75 Clark, *Song*, p.12.

76 Amankulor, 'The Concept and Practice of Traditional African Festival Theatre', Dissertation, University of California, 1977, p.425, quoted by Wetmore, *Black Dionysus,* p.69. Owusu, *Drama of the Gods: A Study of Seven African Plays* (Roxbury: Omenana, 1983), p.88.

77 Clark, *Song*, p.47.

78 Clark, *Song*, p.87.

79 Sophocles, *The Complete Greek Tragedies: Volume II, Sophocles*, trans. David Grene and Richmond Lattimore (Chicago: University of Chicago Press, 1992), p.76.

80 Quoted by Wetmore, *Black Dionysus,* p.64.

81 Clark, *The Example of Shakespeare* (Evanston: Northwestern University Press, 1970), p.24.

82 Clark, *The Example of Shakespeare,* p.83.

83 Clark, 'Aspects of Nigerian Drama', in *African Writers on African Writing,* ed. G.D. Killam (London: Heinemann, 1973), p.20.

84 Clark-Bekederemo, *A Reed in the Tide* (London: Longmans, 1965), p.vii.

85 McLoughlin, 'The Plays of John Pepper Clark', *English Studies in Africa,* 18:1 (1975), 31–40 (p.31).

86 Synge, *The Shadow of the Glen,* in Synge, *Collected Works,* III, 29–62, p.35.

87 Esslin, 'Two African Playwrights', *Black Orpheus,* 19 (March 1966), 33–9 (p.37).

88 Benson, *Black Orpheus, Transition, and Modern Cultural Awakening in Africa* (Berkeley: University of California Press, 1986), pp.60–1.

89 Soyinka, *Myth, Literature and the African World,* pp.46–7.

90 Soyinka, *Myth, Literature and the African World,* p.38.

91 Wetmore, *Black Dionysus,* p.64.

92 Wetmore, *Black Dionysus,* p.3.

93 Wetmore, *Black Dionysus,* p.37.

94 Wetmore, *Black Dionysus,* p.75.

95 Okagbue, 'John Pepper Clark (1935 -)', in *African Writers (Volume II),* ed. Brian Cox (New York: Scribner, 1997), pp.153–66, p.161.

96 Killam and Kerfoot, 'Bekederemo, J(ohn) P(epper) Clark (1935-)', in *Student Encyclopedia of African Literature,* ed. Killam and Kerfoot (Westport: Greenwood, 2008), pp.50–1, p.50.

97 Reiss, 'Tragedy', in *The Princeton Encyclopedia of Poetry and Politics,* ed. Roland Greene et al., 4th edn (Princeton: Princeton University Press, 2012), pp.1446–53, p.1451.

98 Penelope Gilliatt, 'A Nigerian Original', *Observer,* 19 September 1965, p.25.

99   'A Fierce Code Dramatized', *The Times*, 17 September 1965, p.13.

100 McDonald, 'Black Antigone and Gay Oedipus', *Arion: A Journal of Humanities and the Classics*, 17:1 (2009), 25–52 (p.36).

101 Jeyifo, 'Tragedy, History and Ideology', in *Marxism and African Literature*, ed. Georg M. Gugelberger (Trenton: Africa World Press, 1985), pp.94–109, p.96.

102 Fugard, '*Antigone* in Africa', in *Amid Our Troubles*, ed. Marianne McDonald and J. Michael Walton (London: Methuen, 2002), p.132.

103 'Legendary Playwright Athol Fugard Speaks about His Extraordinary Career, His Life and His Regrets', *Sunday Independent*, 21 February 2010 < https://www.pressreader.com/south-africa/the-sunday-independe nt/20100221/282497179819560>.

104 Mshengu, 'Political Theatre in South Africa and the Work of Athol Fugard', *Theatre Research International*, 7:3 (1982), 160–79 (p.178).

105 Errol Durbach, 'Sophocles in South Africa', *Comparative Drama*, 18:3 (1984), 252–64 (p.253).

106 Quayson, *Calibrations* (Minneapolis: University of Minnesota Press, 2003), p.58.

107 Quayson, *Calibrations*, p.59.

108 https://oilspillmonitor.ng

109 Ordinioha and Brisibe, 'The Human Health Implications of Crude Oil Spills in the Niger Delta, Nigeria', *Nigerian Medical Journal*, 54:1 (2013), 10–16 (p.10). <https://www.ncbi.nlm.nih.gov/pmc/articles/PMC3644738/>.

110 Bruederle and Hodler, 'Effect of Oil Spills on Infant Mortality in Nigeria', *PNAS*, 116:12 (2019), 5467–71 (p.5467).

111 Mbajiorgu, *Wake Up Everyone* (Ibadan: Kraftgriots, 2011), p.69, p.64.

112 Mbajiorgu, *Wake Up Everyone*, p.57.

113 Mbajiorgu, *Wake Up Everyone*, p.37, p.59.

114 Mbajiorgu, *Wake Up Everyone,* p.37.

115 Mbajiorgu, *Wake Up Everyone,* p.14.

116 Mbajiorgu, *Wake Up Everyone,* p.59.

117 Mbajiorgu, *Wake Up Everyone,* p.59.

118 Mbajiorgu, *Wake Up Everyone,* p.78.

119 Mbajiorgu, *Wake Up Everyone,* p.77.

120 Scott, 'The Tragic Vision in Postcolonial Time', p.800.

121 Quayson, *Calibrations*, p.74.

Conclusion

1   Clark, *Song*, p.7.

2   Clark, *Song*, p.27, p.2.

3   Malouf, p.147.

4   See, for example, Kovacs, 'Ghosts of Brecht's Women Lay Claim to His Plays', *Independent*, 7 February 1998 <https://www.independent.co.uk/news/ghosts-brecht-s-women-lay-claim-his-plays-1143276.html>: in addition to plagiarizing the writing of those women who were close to him, Brecht is reported to have 'tyrannised women, drove them to suicide and forced them to abort his children'. Walcott, meanwhile, was accused of sexually harassing female students at Harvard and Boston University, which derailed his chance of becoming professor of poetry at Oxford in 2009. See 'Derek Walcott's Acts of Sexual Harassment', *New York Times*, 21 May 2017, <https://www.nytimes.com/2017/03/21/opinion/derek-walcotts-acts-of-sexual-harassment.html>.

5   Kane, *Blasted* (London: Bloomsbury, 2015). Graham Saunders, '"Out Vile Jelly": Sarah Kane's "Blasted" & Shakespeare's "King Lear"', *New Theatre Quarterly*, 20:1 (2004), 69–78 (pp.76–7).

6   Graeae is a group of deaf and disable theatre makers whose members staged a remarkable version of Sarah Kane's *Blasted* in 2006.

7   'The Fourth Stage' originally appeared in *The Morality of Art*,
     ed. D.W. Jefferson (London: Routledge and Kegan Paul, 1969).
     The piece was later reproduced as the final essay in his *Myth,
     Literature and the African World*. See Soyinka, *Myth, Literature
     and the African World*, p.141.

8   Wallace, 'Introduction', in Bushnell et al., VI, 1–21 (p.18).

9   Synge, *Collected Works*, III, 27.

BIBLIOGRAPHY

Aboelazm, Ingy, 'Reworking John Millington Synge's *Riders to the Sea*', 330-2011 2nd International Conference on Humanities, Historical and Social Sciences *IPEDR*, 17 (2011), 330–4

Acampora, Ralph, 'Using and Abusing Nietzsche for Environmental Ethics', *Environmental Ethics*, 16 (1994), 187–94

Adorno, Theodor, *Aesthetic Theory*, ed. and trans. Robert Hullot-Kentor (London: Bloomsbury, 2013)

Adorno, Theodor, 'Cultural Criticism and Society', in *Prisms*, trans. Samuel and Shierry Weber (Cambridge: MIT Press, 1983), pp.17–34

Adorno, Theodor, 'Is Art Lighthearted?', in *Notes to Literature, Volume 2*, trans. Shierry Weber Nicholsen (New York: Columbia University Press, 1992), pp.252–3

Agarwalla, Shyam S., *The African Poetry and Drama* (New Delhi: Prestige, 2000)

Aristophanes, *Frogs*, trans. Alan H. Sommerstein (Warminster: Aris & Phillips, 1996)

Aristophanes, *Thesmophoriazusae*, trans. Alan H. Sommerstein (Warminster: Aris & Phillips, 1994)

Aristotle, *Poetics*, trans. Anthony Kenny (Oxford: Oxford University Press, 2013)

Asanga, Siga, 'Theory and Practice in the Plays of John Pepper Clark and Wole Soyinka', University of Ottowa, PhD thesis, 1978

Banham, Martin, 'Nigerian Dramatists', *Journal of Commonwealth Literature* 7 (1969), 132–6

Banham, Martin, Errol Hill and George Woodyard, eds, *The Cambridge Guide to African and Caribbean Theatre* (Cambridge: Cambridge University Press, 1994), pp.225–48

Beckett, Samuel, *Proust and Three Dialogues with Georges Duthuit* (London: John Calder, 1965)

Beckett, Samuel, *Waiting for Godot*, 2nd edn (London: Faber, 1965)

Benjamin, Walter, *The Origin of German Tragic Drama*, trans. John Osborne (London: Verso, 2003)

Benjamin, Walter, 'What Is Epic Theatre?' [I], in *Understanding Brecht*, trans. Anna Bostock (London: Verso, 2003), pp.1–15

Benjamin, Walter, 'What Is Epic Theatre? (II)', in *Selected Writings*, 4 vols, trans. Edmund Jephcott and Others, ed. Howard Eiland and Michael W. Jennings (Cambridge: Harvard University Press, 2003), IV, 302–12

Benson, Peter, *Black Orpheus, Transition, and Modern Cultural Awakening in Africa* (Berkeley: University of California Press, 1986)

Bohlmann, Otto, *Yeats and Nietzsche* (London: Macmillan, 1982)

Bourgeois, Maurice, *John Millington Synge and the Irish Theatre* (London: Constable, 1913)

Boyd, Ernest, *Ireland's Literary Renaissance* (New York: Barnes & Noble, 1916)

Bradley, A.C., *Shakespearean Tragedy*, 2nd edn (London: Macmillan, 1919)

Brecht, Bertolt, *Brecht on Performance*, ed. Steve Giles et al. (London: Bloomsbury, 2018)

Brecht, Bertolt, *Brecht on Theatre*, ed. Steve Giles et al., rev. 3rd edn (London: Bloomsbury, 2015)

Brecht, Bertolt, *Collected Plays*, ed. John Willett et al., 8 vols (London: Bloomsbury, 2004)

Brecht, Bertolt, 'Key Points in Korsch, pp.37 and 54', in *Brecht on Art and Politics*, ed. and trans. Thomas Kuhn and Steve Giles (London: Methuen, 2003), pp.109–10

Brecht, Bertolt, *Stücke: XI* (Frankfurt am Main: Suhrkamp Verlag, 1959)

Breslin, Paul, *Nobody's Nation* (Chicago: University of Chicago Press, 2001)

Bruchhäuser, Wilfried, *Komponisten der Gegenwart im Deutschen Komponisten-Interessenverband: ein Handbuch* (Berlin: Deutscher Komponisten-Interessenverband, 1995)

Bruederle, Anna, and Roland Hodler, 'Effect of Oil Spills on Infant Mortality in Nigeria', *PNAS*, 116:12 (2019), 5467–71

Bushnell, Rebecca, et al., eds, *A Cultural History of Tragedy*, 6 vols (London: Bloomsbury, 2020)

Callaghan, Dympna, *Woman and Gender in Renaissance Tragedy* (New York and London: Harvester Wheatsheaf, 1989)

Camus, Albert, 'Lecture Given in Athens on the Future of Tragedy', in *Lyrical and Critical Essays*, ed. and trans. Philip Thody (London: Hamish Hamilton, 1967), pp.177–87

Cannon Harris, Susan, 'Mobilizing Maurya', *Modern Drama*, 56:1 (2013), 38–59

Cardullo, Bert, '"Riders to the Sea": A New View', *Canadian Journal of Irish Studies*, 10:1 (1984), 95–112

Casey, Daniel J., 'An Aran Requiem', *Critical Essays on John Millington Synge*, ed. Daniel J. Casey (New York: G.K. Hall, 1994), pp.88–97

Church, Alfred J., *Stories from the Greek Tragedians* (London: Seeley, Jackson & Halliday, 1880)

Clark, J.P., 'Aspects of Nigerian Drama', in *African Writers on African Writing*, ed. G.D. Killam (London: Heinemann, 1973)

Clark, J.P., *The Example of Shakespeare* (Evanston: Northwestern University Press, 1970)

Clark, J.P., *A Reed in the Tide* (London: Longmans, 1965)

Clark, J.P., *Song of a Goat*, J.P. Clark, *Three Plays* (London and Ibadan: Oxford University Press, 1964), pp.1–48

Cohn, Ruby, *Modern Shakespeare Offshoots* (Princeton: Princeton University Press, 1976)

Collini, Stefan. 'The "Tragedy" Paper at Cambridge', *Cambridge Authors* <https://www.english.cam.ac.uk/cambridgeauthors/the-tragedy-paper-continuity-and-change/>

Cooper, Andrew, *The Tragedy of Philosophy* (Albany: State University of New York Press, 2016)

Currey, James, 'Literary Publishing after Nigerian Independence', *Research in African Literatures*, 44:2 (2013), 8–16

Dickson, Keith, *Towards Utopia* (Oxford: Clarendon, 1978)

Drenthen, Martin, 'Wildness as a Critical Border Concept', *Environmental Values*, 14 (2005), 317–37

Durbach, Errol, 'Sophocles in South Africa', *Comparative Drama*, 18:3 (1984), 252–64

Eagleton, Terry, *Sweet Violence: A Study of the Tragic* (Oxford: Blackwell, 2002)

Eagleton, Terry, *Tragedy* (New Haven: Yale University Press, 2020)

Ellis, Sylvia, *The Plays of W.B. Yeats* (Basingstoke: Macmillan, 1995)

Ellmann, Richard, *James Joyce*, rev. edn (Oxford: Oxford University Press, 1982)

Erickson, Jon, 'Is Nothing to Be Done?', *Modern Drama*, 50:2 (2007), 258–75

Esslin, Martin, *Brecht* (London: Eyre Methuen, 1963)

Esslin, Martin, 'Two African Playwrights', *Black Orpheus*, 19 (March 1966), 33–9

Estok, Simon C., 'Doing Ecocriticism with Shakespeare', in *Early Modern Ecostudies*, ed. Thomas Hallock et al. (Houndmills: Palgrave Macmillan, 2008), pp.77–91

Ewen, Frederic, *Bertolt Brecht* (London: Calder & Boyars, 1970)

Falola, Toyin, and Matthew M. Heaton, *A History of Nigeria* (Cambridge: Cambridge University Press, 2008)

Fischer-Lichte, Erika, *Dionysus Resurrection* (Chichester: Wiley-Blackwell, 2014)

Fogarty, Anne, 'Ghostly Intertexts', in *Synge and Edwardian Ireland*, ed. Brian Cliff and Nicholas Grene (Cambridge: Cambridge University Press, 2012), pp.225–43

Fordham, Finn, *Lots of Fun at Finnegans Wake* (Oxford: Oxford University Press, 2007)

Freud, Sigmund, *The Standard Edition of the Complete Psychological Works of Sigmund Freud: Volume IV*, trans. James Strachy (London: Vintage, 2001)

Fugard, Athol, '*Antigone* in Africa', in *Amid Our Troubles*, ed. Marianne McDonald and J. Michael Walton (London: Methuen, 2002)

Garrad, Greg, *Ecocriticism*, 2nd edn (London: Routledge, 2012)

Gerstenberger, Donna, *John Millington Synge* (New York: Twayne, 1965)

Gifford, Denis, *British Film Catalogue: Volume 1*, 3rd edn (London: Routledge, 2001)

Gogarty, Oliver St John, *As I Was Going Down Sackville Street* (London: Rich & Cowan, 1937)

Goldhill, Simon, *Sophocles and the Language of Tragedy* (Oxford: Oxford University Press, 2012)

Goldmann, Lucien, *The Hidden God* (London: Routledge, 1964)

Good, Maeve, *W.B. Yeats and the Creation of a Tragic Universe* (London: Macmillan, 1987)

Gorman, Herbert, *James Joyce: A Definitive Biography* (London: Bodley Head, 1941)

Goulimari, Pelagia, *Literary Criticism and Theory* (Oxford: Routledge, 2015)

Gray, Ronald, 'Brecht and Tragedy', *Cambridge Quarterly*, 8:3 (1979), 236–49

Hall, Edith, *Greek Tragedy* (Oxford: Oxford University Press, 2010)

Hallman, Max, 'Nietzsche's Environmental Ethics', *Environmental Ethics*, 13 (1991), 99–125

Hammond, Brean, *Tragicomedy* (London: Bloomsbury, 2021)

Hammond, Paul, *The Strangeness of Tragedy* (Oxford: Oxford University Press, 2009)

Harari, Yuval, *Sapiens* (London: Harvill Secker, 2014)

Harmsen, Jolien, Guy Ellis, and Robert J. Devaux, *A History of St Lucia* (Vieux Fort: Lighthouse Road, 2012)

Hayman, Ronald, *Brecht* (London: Weidenfeld and Nicolson, 1983)

Hecht, Werner, 'Brecht "und" Beckett', *Theater der Zeit*, 21:14 (August 1966), 28–30

Hegel, G.W.F., *Hegel's Aesthetics: Lectures on Fine Art: Volume 1*, trans. T.M. Knox (Oxford: Clarendon Press, 1975)

Heise, Ursula K., *Sense of Place and Sense of Planet* (Oxford: Oxford University Press, 2008)

Hewitt, Seán, *J.M. Synge: Nature, Politics, Modernism* (Oxford: Oxford University Press, 2021)

Hill, Philip G., ed, *Our Dramatic Heritage: Volume 5* (Rutherford: Fairleigh Dickinson University Press, 1991)

Hirsch, Edward, and Derek Walcott, 'An Interview with Derek Walcott', *Contemporary Literature*, 20:3 (1979), 279–92

Hölderlin, Friedrich, *The Death of Empedocles*, trans. David Farrell Krell (Albany: State University of New York Press, 2008)

Holloway, Joseph, *Joseph Holloway's Abbey Theatre*, ed. Robert Hogan and Michael J. O'Neill (Carbondale: Southern Illinois University Press, 1967)

Innes, Christopher, *Edward Gordon Craig* (Amsterdam: Harwood, 1998)

Ionica, Cristina, *The Affects, Cognition and Politics of Samuel Beckett's Postwar Drama* (Cham: Palgrave Macmillan, 2020)

Jacobs, Nicholas and Prudence Ohlsen, eds, *Bertolt Brecht in Britain* (London: TQ Publications, 1976)

Jameson, Fredric, *Brecht and Method* (London: Verso, 1998)

Jaspers, Karl, *Tragedy Is Not Enough*, trans. H. A. T. Reiche et al. (London: Victor Gollancz, 1953)

Jeyifo, Biodun, 'Tragedy, History and Ideology', in *Marxism and African Literature*, ed. Georg M. Gugelberger (Trenton: Africa World Press, 1985), pp.94–109

Johnson, James Weldon, *God's Trombones: Seven Negro Sermons in Verse* (London: Penguin, 2008)

Johnson, Jonah M., 'Modern Philosophy and Greek Tragedy', in *The Encyclopedia of Greek Tragedy*, ed. Hanna M. Roisman, 3 vols (London: Wiley-Blackwell, 2014), II, 853–59

Joyce, James, *Finnegans Wake* (London: Penguin, 1992)

Joyce, James, *Letters of James Joyce*, ed. Stuart Gilbert and Richard Ellmann, 3 vols (London: Faber, 1957–66)

Joyce, James, *A Portrait of the Artist as a Young Man*, ed. Jeri Johnson (Oxford: Oxford University Press, 2000)

Joyce, Stanislaus, *My Brother's Keeper*, ed. Richard Ellmann (London: Faber, 1957)

Kane, Sarah, *Blasted* (London: Bloomsbury, 2015)

Karl, Korsch, *Kernpunkte der materialistischen Geschichtsauffassung* (Leipzig: C.L. Hirschfeld, 1922)

Kennedy, Joy, 'Sympathy between Man and Nature', *Interdisciplinary Studies in Literature and Environment*, 11:1 (2004), 15–30

Kiberd, Declan, *Inventing Ireland* (London: Jonathan Cape, 1995)

Kiberd, Declan, 'J.M. Synge: "A Faker of Peasant Speech"?', *Review of English Studies*, 30:117 (1979), 59–63

Killam, Douglas and Alicia Kerfoot, 'Bekederemo, J(ohn) P(epper) Clark (1935-)', in *Student Encyclopedia of African Literature*, ed. Douglas Killam and Alicia Kerfoot (Westport: Greenwood, 2008), pp.50–1

King, Bruce, *From New National to World Literature* (Stuttgart: Ibidem, 2016)

Kitcher, Philip, *Joyce's Kaleidoscope* (Oxford: Oxford University Press, 2007)

Knowlson, James, *Damned to Fame* (New York: Simon & Schuster, 1996)

Kruse, Axel, 'Tragicomedy and Tragic Burlesque', *Sydney Studies in English*, 1 (1975), 76–96

Lavrin, Janko, *Nietzsche: An Approach* (London: Routledge, 2010)

Lawrence, D.H., *The Letters of D.H. Lawrence*, ed. James Boulton et al., 8 vols (Cambridge: Cambridge University Press, 1979–2001)

Lawrence, D.H., *The Plays*, ed. Hans-Wilhelm Schwarze and John Worthen, 2 vols (Cambridge: Cambridge University Press, 2002)

Lecossois, Hélène, *Performance, Modernity and the Plays of J.M. Synge* (Cambridge: Cambridge University Press, 2021)

Lehmann, Hans-Thies, *Tragedy and Dramatic Theatre*, trans. Erik Butler (London: Routledge, 2016)

Lloyd, Michael, 'Playboy of the Ancient World?', *Classics Ireland*, 18 (2011), 52–68

Lukács, György, 'The Metaphysics of Tragedy' (1910) in *Soul & Form*, ed. John T. Sanders and Katie Terezakis, trans. Anna Bostock (New York: Columbia University Press, 2010), pp.175–98

Maeterlinck, Maurice, *The Treasure of the Humble*, trans. Alfred Sutro (New York: Dodd, Mead & Company, 1912)

Malouf, Michael, 'Dissimilation and Federation: Irish and Caribbean Modernisms in Derek Walcott's *The Sea at Dauphin*', in *Comparative American Studies: An International Journal*, 8:2 (2010), 140–54 (p.146).

Marlowe, Christopher, *Doctor Faustus, A-Text, Doctor Faustus and Other Plays*, ed. David Bevington and Eric Rasmussen (Oxford: Oxford University Press, 1995), pp.137–83

Marx, Karl, *Grundrisse*, trans. Martin Nicolaus (London: Vintage, 1973)

Masefield, John, *John M. Synge: A Few Personal Recollections, with Biographical Notes* (Dundrum: Cuala Press, 1915)

Masefield, John, *The Tragedy of Nan, and Other Plays* (New York: Macmillan, 1921)

Maxwell, D.E.S., *A Critical History of Modern Irish Drama* (Cambridge: Cambridge University Press, 1984)

Mbajiorgu, Greg, *Wake Up Everyone* (Ibadan: Kraftgriots, 2011)

McCormack, William, *Fool of the Family* (London: Weidenfeld & Nicolson, 2000)

McCrea, Barry, 'Style and Idiom', in *The Cambridge Companion to Irish Modernism*, ed. Joe Cleary (Cambridge: Cambridge University Press, 2014), pp.35–50

McDonald, Marianne, 'Black Antigone and Gay Oedipus', *Arion: A Journal of Humanities and the Classics*, 17:1 (2009), 25–52

McDonald, Rónán, *Tragedy and Irish Literature* (Houndmills: Palgrave, 2002)

McGuinness, Patrick, *Maurice Maeterlinck and the Making of Modern Theatre* (Oxford: Oxford University Press, 2000)

McLoughlin, T.O., 'The Plays of John Pepper Clark', *English Studies in Africa*, 18:1 (1975), 31–40

Meeker, Joseph, *The Comedy of Survival: Studies in Literary Ecology* (New York: Scribner, 1974)

Miller, Arthur, 'Tragedy and the Common Man', *New York Times*, 27 February 1949, p.X1

Mirchandani, Sharon, *Marga Richter* (Urbana: University of Illinois Press, 2012)

Moradiellos, Enrique, *Franco* ([?]: I.B. Tauris, 2017)

Moran, James, *Modernists and the Theatre* (London: Bloomsbury, 2022)

Morash, Christopher, *Yeats on Theatre* (Cambridge: Cambridge University Press, 2021)

Morin, Emilie, *Beckett's Political Imagination* (Cambridge: Cambridge University Press, 2017)

Mshengu, Robert, 'Political Theatre in South Africa and the Work of Athol Fugard', *Theatre Research International*, 7:3 (1982), 160–79

Nadel, Ira, 'Beckett's Holocaust', *The Palgrave Handbook of Holocaust Literature and Culture*, ed. Victoria Aarons and Phyllis Lassner (Cham: Palgrave Macmillan, 2020), pp.697–705

Nchia, Yimbu Emmanuel, '"As It Was in the Beginning …": Religious Fanaticism and the Quest for a New Messiah in the Plays of Derek Walcott and Bate Besong', in *Re-writing Past, Imagining Futures*, ed. Victor N. Gomia and Gilbert S. Ndi (Denver: Spears, 2017), pp.56–71

Nelson, G.E., 'The Birth of Tragedy out of Pedagogy', *The German Quarterly*, 46:4 (1973), 566–80

Newton, K.M., *Modern Literature and the Tragic* (Edinburgh: Edinburgh University Press, 2008)

Nietzsche, Friedrich, *The Birth of Tragedy*, trans. Douglas Smith (Oxford: Oxford University Press, 2000)

Nietzsche, Friedrich, 'Homer's Contest', in '*On the Genealogy of Morality' and Other Writings*, ed. Keith Ansell-Pearson, trans. Carol Diethe (Cambridge: Cambridge University Press, 2007), pp.174–81

Nwakanma, Obi, *Christopher Okigbo, 1930–67* (Woodbridge: James Currey, 2010)

Okagbue, Osita, 'John Pepper Clark (1935-)', in *African Writers (Volume II)*, ed. Brian Cox (New York: Scribner, 1997), pp.153–66

Okagbue, Osita, 'Nigeria', in *The Continuum Companion to Twentieth Century Theatre*, ed. Colin Chambers (London: Continuum, 2002), pp.549–51

Ordinioha, Best and Seiyefa Brisibe, 'The Human Health Implications of Crude Oil Spills in the Niger Delta, Nigeria', *Nigerian Medical Journal*, 54:1 (2013), 10–16

Owusu, Martin, *Drama of the Gods: A Study of Seven African Plays* (Roxbury: Omenana, 1983)

Parker, Stephen, *Bertolt Brecht* (London: Bloomsbury, 2014)

Pavis, Patrice, *Dictionary of the Theatre*, trans. Christine Shantz (Toronto: University of Toronto Press, 1998)

Pilling, John, 'Beckett's *Proust*', *Journal of Beckett Studies*, I (1976), 8–29

Plato, *Republic: Books 6–10*, ed. Chris Emlyn-Jones and William Preddy (Cambridge, MA: Harvard University Press, 2013)

Pomerantsev, Peter, *Nothing Is True and Everything Is Possible* (London: Faber, 2015)

Povey, John, 'West African Drama in English', *Comparative Drama*, 1:2 (1967), 110–21

Quayson, Ato, *Calibrations* (Minneapolis: University of Minnesota Press, 2003)

Quayson, Ato, *Tragedy and Postcolonial Literature* (Cambridge: Cambridge University Press, 2021)

Rabaud, Henri, *L'appel de la mer* (Paris: Max Eschig, 1924)

Rasch, Wolfdietrich, 'Bertolt Brechts marxistischer Lehrer', in *Zur deutschen Literatur seit der Jahrhundertwende, Gesammelte Aufsätze* (Stuttgart: Metzler, 1967)

Reiss, Timothy J., *Against Autonomy* (Stanford: Stanford University Press, 2002)

Reiss, Timothy J., 'Tragedy' in *The Princeton Encyclopedia of Poetry and Politics*, ed. Roland Greene et al., 4th edn (Princeton: Princeton University Press, 2012), pp.1446–53

Richards, I.A., *Principles of Literary Criticism* (London and New York: Routledge, 2001)

Robinson, Courtney J., Brendan J.M. Bohannan, and Vincent B. Young, 'From Structure to Function', *Microbiology and Molecular Biology Reviews*, 74:3 (2010), 453–76

Robinson, Tim, *Stones of Aran: Pilgrimage* (London: Penguin, 1990)

Roche, Anthony, 'Synge, Brecht, and the Hiberno-German Connection', *Hungarian Journal of English and American Studies*, 10:1/2 (2004), 9–32

Rülicke-Weiler, Käthe, *Die Dramaturgie Brechts* (Berlin: Henschelverlag Kunst und Gesellschaft, 1968)

Salter, W.H., *Essays on Two Moderns* (London: Sidgwick & Jackson, 1911)

Sarkar, Nirjhar, 'Existence as Self-making in Derek Walcott's *Sea at Dauphin*', *Anthurium*, 14:2 (2018), 1–13

Sartre, Jean-Paul, *Un théâtre de situations* (Paris: Gallimard, 1973)

Saunders, Graham, '"Out Vile Jelly": Sarah Kane's "Blasted" & Shakespeare's "King Lear"', *New Theatre Quarterly*, 20:1 (2004), 69–78

Schmitt, Natalie Crohn, 'Intimations of Immortality', *Theatre Journal*, 31:4 (1979), 501–10

Schopenhauer, Arthur, 'Supplement I: An Essay on Visions and Matters Connected Therewith', in Richard Wagner, *Beethoven: With a Supplement from the Philosophical Works of Arthur Schopenhauer*, trans. Edward Dannreuther (London: W.M. Reeves, 1903), pp.115–53

Schopenhauer, Arthur, *The World as Will and Representation*, 2 vols, trans. and ed. Judith Norman et al. (Cambridge: Cambridge University Press, 2010–18)

Scott, David, 'The Tragic Vision in Postcolonial Time', *PMLA*, 129:4 (2014), 799–808

Shaw, Bernard, *The Drama Observed: Volume III, 1897–1911*, ed. Bernard F. Dukore (University Park, PA: Pennsylvania State University Press, 1993)

Shaw, Bernard, 'Preface: *The Shewing-up of Blanco Posnet*', in *Playlets*, ed. James Moran (Oxford: Oxford University Press, 2021), pp.217–73

Shaw, Bernard, *The Quintessence of Ibsenism*, in Shaw, *Major Critical Essays* (London: Constable, 1932), pp.1–150

Skelton, Robin, 'The Politics of J.M. Synge', *The Massachusetts Review*, 18:1 (1977), 7–22

Sophocles, *The Complete Greek Tragedies: Volume II, Sophocles*, ed. David Grene and Richmond Lattimore (Chicago: University of Chicago Press, 1992)

Sophocles, *Oedipus at Colonus*, trans. Eamon Grennan and Rachel Kitzinger (Oxford: Oxford University Press, 2005)

Sophocles, *Oedipus the King, Oedipus at Colonus, Antigone*, trans. F. Storr (London: Heinemann, 1912)

Sophocles, *Sophocles: Plays, Oedipus Coloneus*, trans. R.C. Jebb (London: Bristol Classical Press, 2004)

Soyinka, Wole, *Myth, Literature and the African World* (Cambridge: Cambridge University Press, 1976)

Spence, Barry Allen, 'Sophoclean Beckett in Performance', *Skenè: Journal of Theatre and Drama Studies*, 2:2 (2016), 177–201

Steiner, George, *The Death of Tragedy* (London: Faber, 1961)

Steiner, George, *Grammars of Creation* (New Haven: Yale University Press, 2002)

Steiner, George, '*Tragedy, Pure and Simple*', in *Tragedy and the Tragic*, ed. M.S. Silk (Oxford: Clarendon Press, 1996)

Steiner, George, '"Tragedy" Reconsidered', *New Literary History*, 35:1 (2004), 1–15

Surkov, Vladislav, *Almost Zero*, trans. Nino Gojiashvili and Nastya Valentine, Kindle Edition

Synge, J.M., *Collected Works*, 4 vols, ed. Robin Skelton et al. (London: Oxford University Press, 1962–68)

Szondi, Peter, *An Essay on the Tragic*, trans. Paul Fleming (Stanford: Stanford University Press, 2002)

Szondi, Peter, *Theory of the Modern Drama*, ed. and trans. Michael Hays (Cambridge: Polity, 1987)

Taplin, Oliver, *Greek Fire* (New York: Atheneum, 1990)

Thieme, John, *Derek Walcott* (Manchester: Manchester University Press, 1999)

Thomson, Peter, *Brecht: Mother Courage and Her Children* (Cambridge: Cambridge University Press, 1997)

Udo, Reuben K., *Geographical Regions of Nigeria* (Oakland: University of California Press, 1970)

Vaughan Williams, Ralph, *Riders to the Sea* (London: Oxford University Press, 1936)

Walcott, Derek, *Conversations with Derek Walcott*, ed. William Baer (Jackson: University Press of Mississippi, 1996)

Walcott, Derek, *The Sea at Dauphin, Dream on Monkey Mountain and Other Plays* (New York: Farrar, Straus and Giroux, 1971), pp.41–80

Walcott, Derek, *The Sea at Dauphin, Tamarack Review*, 14 (1960), 76–95

Wallace, Jennifer, *Tragedy since 9/11* (London: Bloomsbury, 2020)

Walton, J. Michael, 'Hit or Myth', in *Amid Our Troubles*, ed. Marianne McDonald and J. Michael Walton (London: Methuen, 2002), pp.3–36

Watson, Walter, *The Lost Second Book of Aristotle's Poetics* (Chicago: University of Chicago Press, 2012)

Welch, Robert, *The Abbey Theatre, 1899–1999* (Oxford: Oxford University Press, 1999)

Wetmore, Kevin, *Black Dionysus* (Jefferson: McFarland, 2003)

White, Daniel R. and Gert Hellerich, 'The Ecological Self: Humanity and Nature in Nietzsche and Goethe', *The European Legacy*, 3:3 (1998), 39–61

Williams, Carolyn, 'Melodrama', in *The Cambridge History of Victorian Literature*, ed. K. Flint (Cambridge: Cambridge University Press, 2012), pp.193–219

Williams, Raymond, *Modern Tragedy* (London: Chatto and Windus, 1966)

Williams, Raymond, 'Theatre as a Political Forum', in *Visions and Blueprints*, ed. Edward Timms and Peter Collier (Manchester: Manchester University Press, 1988), pp.307–20

Winkler, John J. and Froma I. Zeitlin, eds, *Nothing to Do with Dionysos?* (Princeton: Princeton University Press, 1990)

Yeats, W.B., *Collected Works*, ed. Richard J. Finneran et al., 14 vols (New York: Scribner, 1990–2008)

Unpublished manuscript sources

Beckett, Samuel, 'Notebook with dark red covers,scribed on the front cover in capitals "WHOROSCOPE", 11 × 17cm, Undated', University of Reading, BC MS 3000/1

Joyce, James, Harry Ransom Center, Joyce collection, box 1 folder 7, J.M. Synge *Riders to the Sea* (1905) translated into Italian by James Joyce and Nicolo Vidacovich, nd, 26pp

Synge, J.M., Trinity College Dublin, MS 4412, 4418, 4413

Yeats, J.B., MS. Holo. 850. & TS signed. 'John Synge is Dead'. New York Public Library, Astor, Lenox and Tilden Foundations Rare Books and Manuscripts Division. Foster-Murphy Collection, box 14

INDEX

Abbey Theatre 31, 85
Adorno, Theodor 6
Aeschylus 2, 33, 83
    Oresteia 15, 18, 82
    Philoctetes 127
Aidoo, Ama Ata
Anowa 118
Ancient Greek tragedy 2–3,
    5, 9, 15–16, 26, 33, 55,
    62–4, 110, 113–14,
    128
Aristotle 9–10, 19, 22, 32,
    44–5, 65–6, 71–4, 93,
    119, 121, 128

Beckett, Samuel 6, 23–4, 80–5
    Happy Days 82
    Waiting for Godot 28, 81–2,
    84–92, 120
Behan, Brendan
    The Quare Fellow 118
Benjamin, Walter 4–5, 22, 77–8,
    93
Black Lives Matter 90
Boer War 15, 16
Bradley, A.C 19, 20
Brecht, Bertolt 45, 61–93, 116,
    128
    Antigone 76–80, 93
    Buying Brass 74–5
    Life of Galileo 76
    Mother Courage 22, 63,
    76

    *The Resistible Rise of Arturo
    Ui* 91
    *Round Heads and Pointy
    Heads* 91
    Saint Joan of the Stockyards
    76
    Señora Carrar's Rifles 28,
    61–74, 85–8, 123–4,
    126
    View of Aristotle 65–6,
    71–4, 93
    View of Beckett 91–2
    View of Shakespeare 75–6
Büchner, Georg
    Woyzeck 75–6

Calderón de la Barca, Pedro
    80
Callaghan, Dympna 7
Camus, Albert 5, 6, 110
Carr, Marina 127
Censorship 14, 33
Chekhov, Anton 12, 22
Christianity 4–5, 14, 58
Church, Alfred J. 33–4
City Dionysia 3
Clark, J.P. 106, 123, 127
    Song of a Goat 29, 107–18,
    121, 126
Coleridge, Samuel Taylor 49
Colonialism 98, 104–5,
    109–11, 118
Craig, Gordon 15–16

Darwin, Charles 14
Dudow, Slatan 61, 72

Eagleton, Terry 8, 24, 28, 42
Eliot, T.S. 18
Engels, Friedrich 14
Esslin, Martin 63, 115–16
Euripides 2, 14–17, 82–3, 113
    Alcestis 18
    The Bacchae 16–17
    Hippolytus 16
    Medea 16, 35, 127
    Trojan Women 16

Franco, Francisco 61, 62
Freud, Sigmund 18–19
Fugard, Athol
    The Island 120
    Klaas and the Devil 119

Goldhill, Simon 76
Goldmann, Lucien 5–6
Graeae theatre company 127
Granville Barker, Harley 16
Gregory, Lady Augusta 31

Hall, Edith 16
Hansberry, Lorraine 12
Harari, Yuval Noah 58–9
Harris, Zinnie 127
Hauptmann, Gerhart
    The Weavers 67–8
Hegel, G.W.F. 3, 11–13, 28, 42,
    63–4, 68, 84, 85
Hill, Erol 97
Hitler, Adolf 61, 77–80
Hölderlin, Friedrich 13, 78
    The Death of Empedocles 35
Holocaust 6, 91
Hussein, Ebrahim
    Kinjeketile 118

Ibsen, Henrik 12, 14, 19–20, 22
    Brand 36
    A Doll's House 53, 87
    Ghosts 116
Irving, Henry 14

Jameson, Fredric 91
Jaspers, Karl 95
Johnson, Boris 90
Joyce, James 43–7, 49

Kane, Sarah 12
    Blasted 127
    Cleansed 127
    Phaedra's Love 127
Knight, G. Wilson 128
Korsch, Karl 65

Lawrence, D.H.
    *The Widowing of
        Mrs Holroyd* 41–2, 45
Lehmann, Hans-Thies 8, 23–4,
    46–7, 55
Lehrstücke 70
Lorca, Federico García
    Blood Wedding 62
Lukács, György 3–4, 96

Maeterlinck, Maurice 22–3,
    42–3, 84
Marx, Karl 14, 28, 58, 63–5,
    68, 86
Masefield, John 40
    The Tragedy of Nan 41
Mbajiorgu, Greg
    Wake Up Everyone 29, 122–4
Mbari Club 107, 111
Meeker, Joseph 25–6, 57
Melodrama 13–14
Miller, Arthur 36, 40
    Death of a Salesman 20–1

Moscow Arts Theatre 89
Murray, Gilbert 16, 17
Mussolini, Benito 61

New Company (Whitehall) 97
Nietzsche, Friedrich 3, 12, 13,
    28, 49–51, 53–4, 57, 128

Oil industry 121–4

Parks, Suzan-Lori 12, 127
Pavis, Patrice 2
Piscator, Erwin 71
Plato 9
Poel, William 17
Putin, Vladimir 88

Queen Victoria 14
Quayson, Ato 24, 102, 105–6,
    120–1, 124

Racine, Jean 36
Richards, I.A. 8
Romney, Mitt 90
Royal Court Theatre 16

Saro-Wiwa, Ken 120–1
Sartre, Jean-Paul 6–7
Schopenhauer, Arthur 12–13,
    80–1, 83–4, 86–7
Scott, David 24–5, 96, 110, 124
Second World War 22, 66, 73,
    77–80, 91
Seneca 11
Shakespeare 5, 11, 13, 17, 19,
    20, 75, 110
    Hamlet 18, 35, 43, 76, 89,
        127
    King Lear 15, 67, 113, 127
    Macbeth 26, 76
    Othello 43, 83

Richard III 83–4
Romeo and Juliet 83, 113
Shaw, Bernard 14–15, 17, 19
Skantze, P.A. 7
Sophocles 2, 76
    Antigone 11–13, 26, 51,
        76–80, 113, 120
    Oedipus at Colonus 12, 18,
        39, 66–7, 81, 82, 113
    Oedipus Rex 9, 14, 17,
        18–19, 33, 66–7, 72, 81,
        101, 113, 122, 127
    Women of Trachis 83
Soyinka, Wole 107, 109, 111,
    112, 116, 119, 128
    Bacchae 118
Spanish Civil War 22, 61–2,
    69–71, 85
Steiner, George 1–2, 3, 21, 24,
    35, 36, 38, 58, 75, 82,
    96
Storr, Francis 39
Strindberg, August 12, 22
Surkov, Vladislav 88–9
Synge, J.M. 123
    Experiential nature of his
        drama 47
    Hodgkin's disease 32
    Political aspects 38, 110
    Riders to the Sea 27–9,
        31–60, 62–3, 65–6, 68–9,
        73–4, 78, 85–6, 99–106,
        109–12, 118, 120, 122,
        125–6, 129
    In the Shadow of the Glen
        37, 115
Szondi, Peter 22–3

Tansi, Sony Labour
    La parenthèse de sang 118
Taplin, Oliver 95

Tragique quotidien 23–4, 28, 42
Trauerspiel 5
Tree, Herbert Beerbohm 14

Walcott, Derek 45, 96, 123, 127
   The Sea at Dauphin 29,
     97–106, 126
Wallace, Jennifer 7, 129
Weigel, Helene 72–3
Williams, Raymond 21–2, 88, 96
Wordsworth, William 49

Yeats, W.B. 17, 31, 33, 36, 44,
   54–5, 58
   The Dreaming of the Bones
     56
   Fighting the Waves 57
   At the Hawk's Well 26–7,
     55–6
   King Oedipus 81
   Oedipus at Colonus 81
   The Only Jealous of Emer
     57